CULTURE SHOCK!

Chicago

At Your Door

Orin Hargraves

Graphic Arts Center Publishing Company
Portland, Oregon

In the same series

Australia	Hong Kong	Pakistan	Jakarta at Your Door
Bolivia	India	Philippines	London at Your Door
Borneo	Indonesia	Singapore	Paris at Your Door
Britain	Iran	South Africa	Rome at Your Door
Burma	Ireland	Spain	
California	Israel	Sri Lanka	A Globe-Trotter's Guide
Canada	Italy	Sweden	A Parent's Guide
Chile	Japan	Switzerland	A Student's Guide
China	Korea	Syria	A Traveller's Medical Guide
Cuba	Laos	Taiwan	A Wife's Guide
Czech	Malaysia	Thailand	Living and Working Abroad
Republic	Mauritius	Turkey	Working Holidays Abroad
Denmark	Mexico	UAE	
Egypt	Morocco	USA	
France	Nepal	USA—The	
Germany	Netherlands	South	
Greece	Norway	Vietnam	

Illustrations by TRIGG
Photographs from Orin Hargraves

This book is published by special
arrangement with Times Editions Pte Ltd
Times Centre, 1 New Industrial Road, Singapore 536196
International Standard Book Number 1-55868-424-7
Library of Congress Catalog Number 98-87495
Graphic Arts Center Publishing Company
P.O. Box 10306 • Portland, Oregon 97296-0306 • (503) 226-2402

Printed in Singapore

For Paul Pierron,
longtime Chicagoan and longtime friend
who always keeps me coming back for more.

CONTENTS

CHICAGO

NORTH DAKOTA

SOUTH DAKOTA

NEBRASKA

KANSAS

OKLAHOMA

TEXAS

MINNESOTA

WISCONSIN

IOWA

ILLINOIS

MISSOURI

ARKANSAS

LOUISIANA

Chicago

INDIANA

KENTUCKY

TENNESSEE

MISSISSIPPI

ALABAMA

GEORGIA

OHIO

WEST VIRGINIA

VIRGINIA

NORTH CAROLINA

SOUTH CAROLINA

FLORIDA

MICHIGAN

NEW YORK

PENNSYLVANIA

L. Superior

L. Huron

L. Michigan

L. Ontario

L. Erie

St. Lawrence

Missouri

Mississippi

Illinois

Ohio

Mississippi

Rio Grande

Gulf of Mexico

ATLANTIC OCEAN

CHAPTER ONE

WELCOME TO CHICAGO

Hog butcher for the world,
Tool maker, stacker of wheat,
Player with railroads and the nation's freight handler;
Stormy, husky, brawling,
City of the big shoulders.

—Carl Sandburg, *Chicago*

Great cities the world over have a way of working their way into the popular imagination, where they suffer an inevitable reduction: New York is skyscrapers, London is Big Ben, Moscow is the Kremlin. Ask the man on the street about Chicago and you may well get an imitation of a gangland shoot-out, for nothing seems

7

to persist more vividly about the city than its past during the days of Prohibition, and the romance (if you could call it that) of underworld figures like Al Capone and John Dillinger. A visit to Chicago today will quickly dispel the myths that persist about it. You will very likely arrive via the world's busiest airport (O'Hare International), in a city that has:

- three of the world's ten tallest buildings (the Sears Tower, the Standard Oil Building, the John Hancock Center)
- 15 miles of beaches (on Lake Michigan)
- the world's largest public library (the Harold Washington Library Center)
- the world's largest exhibition and convention complex (McCormick Place)
- the university with the greatest number of Nobel Laureates associated with it (the University of Chicago)
- the largest collection of Impressionist paintings outside the Louvre (at the Art Institute)
- the only river in the world that flows backwards (the Chicago River)

But neither myths nor superlatives go very far in acquainting a newcomer with the reality of living and working in a city. For that you need to find out about the real Chicago, only parts of which manage to penetrate the gloss of tourist brochures and other promotional literature. This book is a modest but sincere attempt to set you on the right path to making yourself at home in Chicago. No city of its size in North America offers such an attractive balance of big-city savvy, excellent and varied recreational facilities, and down-to-earth people. And no other book will tell you as much as you need to know about settling down in the place as this one.

To begin, we will try to locate Chicago: where it exists in the minds of Americans and Chicagoans, and more prosaically, where it exists on the map.

A TALE OF THREE CITIES

One of Chicago's enduring nicknames, *Second City*, derives from the fact that for many years it was the second largest city in the United States and regarded by many as always holding a rather faint candle to New York, the undisputed first American city. The second half of the 20th century has seen that pattern gradually and irrevocably changed: with the growth of Los Angeles, Chicago has moved to a distinct third place in population, a position that is not likely to change. But cities should not be judged solely on the size of their population. We have already seen a list of Chicago superlatives. Today it can still lay claim to the epithet *Second City* in many important respects. It is second only to Los Angeles (and ahead of New York) in the volume of many important areas of retail trade, including sales of most consumer goods, food, cars, hardware, and gasoline, and it beats LA (being second only to New York) in apparel sales. And while New York is considered the preeminent financial capital of the Americas, it can't be overlooked that 80 percent of the world's commodity trade takes place in Chicago, primarily via the Chicago Board of Trade and the Chicago Mercantile Exchange, which are only two of Chicago's five major financial markets.

It is easy to make the argument that Chicago has lost out to Los Angeles and New York because the latter are both coastal cities and enjoy distinct advantages in terms of international trade and tourism. No figures dispute this. New York and Los Angeles enjoy vastly more shipping trade and international tourism than Chicago, despite the fact that Chicago is an inland port and has excellent international air connections. But you will probably not find a Chicagoan who thinks that Chicago has "lost out" on anything that really matters because of this. Whatever attractions the coastal cities may hold, Chicago has lost nothing to them in terms of quality of life. It ranks far above both Los Angeles and New York in published surveys that measure the various social,

9

economic, and cultural factors that contribute to the overall well-being of people in American cities. Most notably, Chicago has a significantly lower rate of violent crime than either Los Angeles or New York.

Chicago has been historically, and still is a capital of the land: the magnet for the largely agricultural Midwest, as well as the hub of North America's rail, road, and air transportation. Chicago was settled by and is still largely inhabited by people whose roots are in the land. For that reason it has a distinctly different feel than either of America's largest coastal cities: more down-to-earth, more businesslike, more friendly, and more modest. Actor Michael Douglas summed up the feeling well in his observation: "I like Chicago. New York is talk. Los Angeles is hype. Chicago is work."

ZEROING IN ON CHICAGO

It's probably not possible to feel really grounded in Chicago without having an idea of where you are in relation to everything else. To help you get your bearings, we'll take a look at the geography of Chicago, starting with a bird's-eye view and slowly narrowing our focus until we come to the heart of the city and an explanation of its local geography and the layout of its streets.

Chicago is the port closest to the heart of North America, although many are surprised to hear that it is a port at all. In fact, the Great Lakes are accessible to ocean-going ships. They pass through the St. Lawrence Seaway, the system of locks, canals, and lakes that connects the St. Lawrence River to Lake Ontario. The Seaway is closed to shipping in the frozen winter months but is a busy conduit for trade at all other times of year and allows Chicago to compete with some coastal ports in international trade.

Americans think of Chicago as being situated in the **Midwest**. A look at the map will show you that Chicago is in fact nearer the east than the west coast of the United States, but early settlement patterns resulted in the entire middle section of the country being thought of as the West. Gradually, as settlement moved even farther westward, the middle of the country became known as the Midwest. Another popular term for this part of the country is **America's Heartland**, partly because it is in the middle of the country but also because it has been historically the agricultural center on which the rest of the United States depends. Chicago is undeniably the capital of the Midwest and of the Heartland; it attracts the best and brightest from all over the Midwest where state economies are still largely agricultural, although with a sizable amount of manufacturing. A smaller regional designation for the area of Chicago is the **Great Lakes region**: the states that border the Great Lakes, including Wisconsin, Michigan, Ohio, Indiana, Illinois, and the western parts of New York and Pennsylvania. Chicago stretches out along the southwestern shore of **Lake Michigan**, second largest of the Great Lakes.

On a smaller scale, Chicago is located in the state of **Illinois**. It is not the capital of the state (Springfield is), but it so dominates the life of the state (in the minds of some, anyway) that its presence gives rise to the term "**downstate**," meaning all the parts of Illinois that are not part of the Chicago area. In fact nearly two-thirds of the state's residents live within a couple of hours' drive of Chicago, which sprawls across the northeast corner of Illinois.

The collective term for Chicago and all of its far-reaching suburbs is **Chicagoland.** This term describes an area with fluid boundaries; it has various meanings depending on the intent of the speaker. In its grandest application, it takes in 3,800 square miles (9,840 sq. km), encompassing 265 different municipalities, parts of six Illinois counties and parts of three states (northwest Indiana and southeast Wisconsin, in addition to Illinois). In principle, Chicagoland includes anyplace from which a person could reasonably commute to downtown Chicago to work, and this area

11

has been growing for the past 50 years. Many towns that were initially remote from Chicago and grew as independent communities are now part of its suburbs.

Within Chicagoland the political boundaries include counties and municipalities (which may be officially called cities, towns, villages, or townships). The **City of Chicago** is entirely within **Cook County**, which runs along Lake Michigan and inland from the lake for a few miles. Several of Chicago's suburbs are within Cook County, but the surrounding counties, DuPage, Kane, Lake, McHenry, and Will, also consist almost entirely of Chicago suburbs, with the odd industrial area, nature conservation area, or rare undeveloped area interspersed. This group of counties is occasionally called the **six-county area** for demographic purposes. Each suburb of Chicago is an incorporated city, town, or village with its own, usually not unique, set of laws and regulations that apply only within its borders. Adjacent suburbs tend to differ very little from each other in most respects and often the only way you know that you're going from one to another is that the style of street signs changes.

Within the city of Chicago there are two kinds of divisions: **wards** and **precincts**, which are political divisions that form the constituencies for local government, and **neighborhoods**, which are informal divisions but are really much more meaningful than any other division within the city. Chicago is often called "a city of neighborhoods" and the neighborhood that you live in very largely colors and flavors your day-to-day life in Chicago. For that reason we will treat neighborhoods in more detail in chapter 4, when we start looking for a place to live.

For navigational purposes, you can think of Chicago as being divided along the lines of the compass: its streets are a precise grid pattern with alignment of major streets running strictly north-south and east-west (see the grid map on page 28). We will examine the grid in more detail a little further on, but it is useful now to

A food giveaway in the Loop — where Chicagoans and tourists are most likely to rub shoulders.

note the major divisions of the city and the images they conjure up for Chicagoans. The names of Chicago's major divisions are in many cases prosaic, but they carry baggage that it is useful to know how to unpack.

In the very heart of Chicago is the **Loop**, named for the elevated train track that forms a one-half square mile loop where the rail lines converge. The area includes everything between Lake Street on the north, Van Buren Street on the south, Wells Street on the west, and Wabash Avenue on the east. The Loop is the central business district, which can also be referred to loosely as **downtown**. It consists largely of stores and offices. For many years the area had a slightly deserted feel on weekends, but there is now a trend to convert underused skyscrapers to residential use, and the Loop is becoming more residential. Slightly east of downtown Chicago is Lake Michigan; the shoreline runs from northwest to southeast. For this reason there is no proper east side of Chicago, though there is a city in northwest Indiana, well within the boundaries of Chicagoland, called East Chicago.

Chicago's business district extends a short distance both north and south of the Loop, and these areas are called the **Near North Side** and **Near South Side** respectively. They are also full of shops and businesses, but have more residential space than the Loop, most of it in the form of fairly pricey condominiums and high-rise apartments. The Near South Side is a relatively recent urban development and is not quite so fashionable as the Near North Side, which is where most of Chicago's deep wealth is concentrated.

The **North Side,** which includes all of Chicago from the Near North to the city limits at Howard Street, is in general terms the most fashionable area of the city. It is largely residential, with the more expensive neighborhoods concentrated along the lakefront. The lakefront is the haunt of young urban professionals, although they certainly don't enjoy a monopoly; among the other sorts of residents are senior citizens, families, and many and various ethnic communities. The **Northwest Side** and the **Southwest Side** are in many ways similar to each other, largely residential for middle-class and working-class families, again with many and varied ethnic enclaves, which are common in Chicago. The **West Side** and the **South Side** are the two areas of Chicago that are mainly black, relatively poor, and filled with substandard public housing. These areas have the highest crime rates in the city.

GEOGRAPHY AND CLIMATE

Chicago lies roughly at 42 degrees north latitude, making it northerly as large cities go, but by no means at an extreme. It is about the same distance from the equator as Beijing and Istanbul and farther south than London or Paris. Being at a relatively high latitude, the length of day varies in Chicago by about six hours:

summer's longest day has more than 15 hours of daylight, winter's shortest day has nine hours.

Chicago is in the Central time zone of the United States, which is five hours earlier than Greenwich Mean Time (GMT) from roughly April through October (when Daylight Savings Time is observed), and six hours earlier than GMT during the winter months. For practical purposes it is six hours behind London at all times of year, barring the odd few days when people on either side of the Atlantic don't turn the clocks forward or back on the same weekend. The time in Chicago is always one hour earlier than New York and other East Coast cities; it is two hours later than Los Angeles and other West Coast cities. It shares the same time zone with Dallas and Houston.

But for the gigantic expanse of Lake Michigan (see below), the physical geography of the city and surrounding area is in every way unexceptional; the elevation at the shore of the lake is 577 feet (176 m) above sea level and doesn't vary by more than a hundred feet within the city. There are no appreciable hills or valleys until you are well beyond Chicago and its near suburbs. Chicago's waterways have been altered considerably from their natural courses to serve the needs of man. The Chicago River ends at Lake Michigan just north of the Loop but does not actually flow into it as it once did; its flow was reversed by the Army Corps of Engineers to prevent the pollution of Chicago's drinking water, taken from the lake. Watercourses on the south side of the city now form a network of canals and artificial lakes called the Illinois Waterway that constitutes part of Chicago's inland maritime port and serves to connect the Great Lakes with the Mississippi River system.

Chicago Seasons

Three cities in the world with a population of more than 5 million typically experience summer temperatures higher than 100°F (38°C) and winter temperatures lower than 0°F (–18°C). The cities

15

are Moscow, Beijing, and Chicago. Chicago's climate is one of extremes, and one with every conceivable type of weather between these extremes. The records for Chicago's hottest ever (104°F) and coldest ever (−4°F) day were in fact set within five months of each other in 1995. But you can often experience some version of the extremes in the same day! Anyone with more than a year's experience in Chicago has probably experienced the arrival of a cold front from the north or northwest that caused temperatures to plummet twenty to thirty degrees in an hour. A rarer but more welcome event is of temperatures rising through the night, when a warmer front from the south or west displaces a cold front in winter.

Although sometimes unpredictable in particulars, the larger pattern of weather throughout the year goes more or less like this: **spring** generally arrives in Chicago by fits and starts in late March but doesn't seem prepared to stay until May, so it is usually a rather short season. In March and April frequent and severe returns to the worse kind of winter weather occur (snow, ice, and strong winds). By May most of these nasty surprises are finished, leaves are out on the trees, and daytime temperatures are pleasant (high 60s and low 70s F). This pattern continues until roughly

the middle of June, when **summer** usually settles in to stay. Summer weather patterns vary in duration but usually follow fixed themes. There are days or weeks of hot and humid weather, coming from the south or southwest, punctuated often by sudden and violent thunderstorms. This pattern is displaced (temporarily) by welcome cooler, drier air coming from the northwest, though this transition is often heralded by violent rain and electrical storms. During hot periods daytime temperatures can stay in the 90s F (high 30s C), with nights only cooling off to the 70s F (mid-20s C). The more pleasant, drier summer weather from the northwest has daytime temperatures in the 80s F (high 20s C) and nights in the low 60s or high 50s (high teens C). Note that preference is given here to the Fahrenheit scale, because that's the one used by weather forecasters and most Americans.

The first hints of **autumn** (or **fall** as Americans call it) normally arrive in Chicago in September in the form of a cool front from the northwest that is cooler and more persistent than the summer ones. Nighttime temperatures dip into the low 50s F (low teens C). Daytime temperatures remain pleasant (70s F) for the most part and sunshine is still plentiful. The pattern continues, regularly alternating with real summerlike weather, into October, with cooler and rainy weather becoming more dominant. Leaves start to change color, though usually not spectacularly in and around Chicago. Around this time of year there is also a nebulous season called **Indian summer**, of indefinite duration, which seems like a return to full-blown summer after autumn has unmistakably arrived.

The days continue to grow shorter, noticeably so by October, and by November the last vestiges of summer are gone. Leaves lie in brown heaps on the ground and chill winds blow. It is this time of year that Chicago lives up to its sobriquet the *Windy City*. The winds that bring the cold weather continue with little respite until late spring. You will become familiar with the term *wind chill*

17

index, which refers to the effective temperature, always lower than the actual temperature, determined by taking the chilling properties of the wind into account. On the coldest days (which, perversely, are often the windiest as well) the wind chill index can drop so low that it is in fact hazardous to expose your bare skin to the air.

Though **winter** doesn't officially begin until late December, the feeling of winter settles into Chicago in November for its long stay. Most weather comes from the northwest and it is mostly cold. Snow is likely to start in November, though none may accumulate until December or even January. Throughout the winter temperatures can vary widely depending on the source of the dominant weather system and whether cloud cover is present or not, but average high temperatures hover right near the freezing point, with nighttime lows averaging well below freezing from December to February. On average, the temperature is at or below freezing in Chicago more than one-third of the days in the year; it's a far cry from the Tropics.

There isn't a "rainy season" in Chicago; precipitation can fall at any time of year. The average yearly precipitation is about 33 inches. By contrast, London, with its reputation for wetness, gets only 29 inches. Wet weather in Chicago comes in relatively concentrated bursts that then move on and make way for sunshine. The sunniest months are typically June, July, and August, when it is reasonable to expect sunshine well over half the days; the gloomiest months are November and December, with sunshine less than half the days.

The Lake and the Weather

Lake Michigan has a marked effect on the weather, and overall a benevolent one. The lake mitigates heat in the summer: temperatures at the lakefront can be as much as 10 degrees (average 5 degrees) cooler than a few miles inland. Similarly in the winter, the lakefront can be marginally warmer, since the lake remains warmer in the winter than the land. So if you think you might find Chicago's weather extremes a bit taxing, you may want to consider living as near the lake as possible. The only downside is the occasional phenomenon called **lake effect snow**, when snowfall is heavier near the lake because of infrequent easterly winds, and the occasional eastern-driven storm that can cause the lake to flood the land and even occasionally close Lake Shore Drive. But these events are the exception rather than the rule, and the lake generally has an improving effect on the weather.

HISTORY

The history of Chicago is rich in detail and is documented in many places at more length than is possible here. For a lively overview and a place to locate all the tools you'll need to discover the endless details, you can't do better than to visit the **Chicago Historical Society (www.chicagohistory.org)**, 1600 N. Clark Street, at the corner of North Avenue. It's the Society's headquarters, but also a museum with permanent and special exhibits, as well as frequent film screenings and other events. Another very good overview of landmark events is the Chicago Public Library's Chronological History of Chicago, on the web at **cpl.lib.uic.edu.** Some of the most important points of Chicago's history that contribute to its current flavor are summarized here.

Chicago's history and phenomenal growth can be summed up in two clichés—first, the motto of the real estate agent: "Location is everything!", and second, the self-evident "Nothing succeeds like success." The point on Lake Michigan where Chicago now stands was a crossroads for Native Americans long before the New World was even a twinkle in the European's eye. When Europeans first journeyed inland—the honors going to the French explorers Joliet and Marquette in 1673—the Native Americans in the area, of the Sauk, Mesquakie, and Potawatomi

19

tribes, had already staked out the area for its strategic location at the intersection of trade routes. One legend has it that it was the Native Americans who showed Marquette and Joliet what they were looking for: a portage that would connect the Atlantic Ocean with the Gulf of Mexico. Most of the pieces were already in place in the form of the Mississippi River and the St. Lawrence River flowing out of the Great Lakes; it remained only to find a way from the southern end of Lake Michigan to the Illinois River and thence to the Mississippi. This was the key to Chicago's early success; it lay right in the path of this portage. For the next hundred years the location continued as a trading post for the French and British fur trade.

The first permanent settler was a trader, Jean Baptiste Point du Sable, from the Caribbean island of Hispañola. He established a trading post on the north bank of the Chicago River in 1779. Prefiguring Chicago's place as one of the great multicultural and multiethnic cities of the world, du Sable was a Catholic of mixed French and African ancestry, who married a Native American woman.

Chicago's history as a permanent settlement begins only at the beginning of the 19th century, with the establishment of Fort Dearborn (its original location is marked in the pavement near the corner of Michigan Avenue and Wacker Drive). Fort Dearborn was built to protect trade routes in an early exercise of authority by the fledgling United States government. By this time the local Native American population had already ceded to the federal government the land on which the fort stood, as well as the surrounding area that is now downtown Chicago. The ceding of land by Native Americans was the key to European settlement of the area around Chicago; once trade routes were under settlers' control, security against native attacks became less and less of an issue and more settlers arrived. Fort Dearborn was eventually closed and Chicago was on its way to becoming a big city.

During the 19th century Chicago's phenomenal growth was fueled by several factors: the move west by settlers looking for land and opportunity; immigration from Europe, which was increasing as people from the Old World became irresistibly drawn to the New; and the development of what were then more modern forms of transportation, namely railroads and canals. These forces combined to start Chicago on the way to being one of the Western world's preeminent cities in a remarkably short time. From a fort at the beginning of the century, Chicago had a population of 30,000 by 1850; of this number, half were born abroad, with Irish and German immigrants comprising the largest group, followed by others from the British Isles, Scandinavia, and France. Chicago's unprecedented growth was described by one early visitor as "one of the most amazing things in the history of modern civilization." Another foreign visitor remarked, "See two things in the United States if nothing else — Niagara Falls and Chicago."

By mid-century, Chicago was established as the rail hub of the westward-expanding United States, as well as a central distribution point for livestock, grain, and lumber. The Union Stockyards, a vast livestock market, opened in 1865 as the largest of its kind in the world (it was in continuous operation until 1971). Livestock arrived in Chicago by rail to be slaughtered and processed in the stockyards. It remains today only in memory, in the area of the southwest side called "Stockyards."

The demand for suitable infrastructure fueled by seemingly unstoppable immigration meant that Chicago looked like a construction site for much of the time from the mid-19th century onward. Amenities did not always keep pace with the need for them, and residents often had to tolerate dire living conditions. Early Chicago was built more or less at ground level, meaning that it was a sea of mud for much of the year when rains caused the lake and river waters to rise and spill into the streets. Drinking water drawn from Lake Michigan became increasingly unsanitary as it

21

was mingled with sewage, and waterborne pestilence reached alarming levels. But the natives found ingenious ways of solving the problem: the entire level of the city was raised, starting around 1855, to bring it up out of the mud. Entire buildings were jacked up and their foundations raised. Eventually the level of streets and sidewalks was high and dry. In 1867 a remarkable engineering feat resulted in a two-mile tunnel that brought fresh water from the middle, rather than from the shores of the lake. This sort of imaginative response to challenge has become a hallmark of Chicago and continues to this day. The motto of the city is, "I will"—and it does.

The singular challenge that faced Chicagoans in the 19th century was rebuilding after the great fire of 1871. The fire, which began in the now legendary barn of Mrs. O'Leary on the southwest side, claimed 300 lives, left 90,000 people homeless, and destroyed $200 million worth of property. But the fire provided the opportunity for the world's architects to design a new city. The first skyscraper, the Home Insurance Building, was erected in Chicago in 1885. Chicago remains today a mecca of modern architecture with many noted historical and contemporary buildings. It could well be argued that Chicago has razed more architectural monuments than many cities have still standing.

Chicago's official status as a world city was sealed with the opening of the Columbian Exposition of 1893, a world's fair commemorating the 400th anniversary of the landing of Columbus. In its six-month run, 27 million people visited the attractions. Most of the extraordinary buildings erected to house the fair exist now only in photographs, but an exceptional one remains, the current Museum of Science and Industry in Hyde Park. The first Ferris wheel was erected at the exposition. Other American icons that made their first appearance at the fair and that can still be found on supermarket shelves today are Cracker Jack, Aunt Jemima syrup, Cream of Wheat, and Juicy Fruit gum.

In 1909 the Chicago Plan was published. Primarily the brain-child of architect Daniel Burnham (whom the harbor is named for), it was the first comprehensive outline for the development of an American city and served to cement Chicago's place as an architectural capital and showplace. The plan called for the beautifcation of the city through the building of parks and recreational spaces and the development of artery roads connecting different sections of the city. Evidence of the plan's effects are still visible today.

In 1933 Chicago hosted yet another world's fair, this one called the Century of Progress, commemorating the 100th anniversary of the incorporation of the city. Its theme was the progress of science and civilization in the hundred years that Chicago had existed. The fair was extended a second summer, partly because of its popularity but also to raise revenue to clear the debts it had accumulated. Thirty-nine million people visited the exposition.

The modern history of Chicago is more or less contained in a single, long-running event: the administration of Mayor Richard J. Daley, who was elected in 1955 and served as mayor until his death in office in 1976. The appearance, infrastructure, and administration of the city today is largely a product of work done while he was in office, and most of what has happened since then could be described as footnotes to his legacy. A Chicago native of sturdy Irish Catholic stock from the neighborhood of Bridgeport, Daley worked his way up from the grass roots of city politics to eventually take the helm of city government. Complaints about the vast and unstoppable political machine that ran Chicago under Daley were as long-running as the administration itself, but in fact the Mayor enjoyed widespread popular support during most of his terms in office and died a local hero. In the period from 1976 to 1989 Chicago had five mayors, none distinguished with the exception of Harold Washington, elected in 1983. He was Chicago's first black mayor and had he not died in office like his mentor Mayor Daley, he might well have left an enduring

The Claes Oldenberg baseball bat, one of the many outdoor works of modern art in Chicago that were erected during Mayor Richard J. Daley's administration.

mark on the city. Chicago's current mayor, in office since 1989, is Richard M. Daley—the eldest son of Richard J. Times have changed: the days of the Democratic Party machine are over, though it could be said that the current Mayor Daley drives a reconditioned, more broadly-based and politically correct version of his father's creation.

ECONOMY

The Midwest is one of the main agricultural centers of the United States; parts of it bear names such as the wheat belt, the bread belt, and the corn belt. While Chicago is a major center for the transport and distribution of agricultural products (13 million bushels of grain can be stored in elevators on Lake Calumet), its own economy is quite diversified. Manufacturing is the most important sector, but it also has key sectors devoted to business services, tourism, high technology, metals, publishing, and health and medical supplies, to name a few.

As the Midwest's commercial, financial, industrial, and cultural center, Chicago has an economy that seems unstoppable in the best of times and remains robust even in economic downturns. Economic sectors that are expected to show the most growth through the first few years of the millennium are also well established in Chicago: real estate, insurance, finance, healthcare, and business services. About 40 of the Fortune 500 companies (the 500 largest in the United States, including several multinationals) have their headquarters in Chicagoland. For this reason, and also because of its excellent transportation network, its proximity to suppliers, and its skilled labor force, Chicago ranks high among the world's cities (in the top ten) as a desirable location for a business. In 1996 Chicago was the top destination of professional workers relocated from other parts of the United States.

The heart of Chicago's financial world are its five major exchanges: the Chicago Board of Trade (CBOT), the Chicago

Mercantile Exchange (CME), the Chicago Board Options Exchange, the Mid-America Commodity Exchange, and the Midwest Stock Exchange. Anyone who doubts the importance and vitality of these financial markets to the American economy should take the opportunity to view their activities. You can visit the public gallery of the Chicago Board of Trade (located in the Loop at La Salle and Jackson) where traders in financial and commodity futures use the "open outcry" system to determine prices, and create an atmosphere as lively as any third world market.

POLITICAL MACHINERY

The various political and governmental entities that control Chicago and Chicagoland will be looked at in more detail in a later chapter, but a brief overview is useful here. The ascending order of authority is: city, county, state, and country. Representative government is the rule at each level, and there are elected officials, statutory bodies, and legislatures that promulgate the will of the people (in theory, anyway) at every level. Municipalities (that is, cities, towns, and villages, including Chicago and all of its many suburbs) typically have an elected city council and a chief executive called a mayor. Counties have the least direct influence in people's lives, but they provide some social services, operate some courts, and in the case of Cook County, operate a major hospital. Chicagoland covers six counties; Cook County is the main one and the one that completely contains the city of Chicago.

The state of Illinois has a popularly elected governor and a house and senate that mirror the U.S. House of Representatives and Senate. Chicago and its suburbs, though remote from state government in Springfield, dominate it in many ways, and conflicts between Chicago and "downstate" interests are frequent, though usually not bitter or intransigent. The city of Chicago has traditionally been, and probably will continue to be, a bastion of the Democratic Party. The suburbs of Chicago are mixed, with the wealthier suburbs typically being Republican overall. As elsewhere in American politics, these two parties dominate all affairs to the near exclusion of any others.

LANDMARK STATUS

We conclude this brief introductory chapter with an orientation guide that will help you to locate the main features of Chicagoland. As in every city, Chicagoans use place names and landmarks as a shorthand way of identifying a place or giving directions. If you know what the main features are and where they are, you'll be on your way to developing a mental map of the city that will help you to feel at home.

Negotiating the Grid

Chicago is laid out on a rectangular grid and oriented toward the cardinal points of the compass. If you're not used to thinking and talking in terms of North, South, East, and West, now is a good time to start, because it makes Chicago very easy to negotiate. (If you're not used to the American system of measure, now is a good time to start learning that too, because distances are figured everywhere in miles.) House numbers are all assigned with reference to a central axis, so a house number not only identifies a house, it tells you roughly where it is in relation to the center of the city. Take a little time to internalize the main points of the house numbering system; then it will be nearly impossible for you to be lost in Chicago, and you will be able to give or understand directions to any address in the city.

Chicago is divided into quadrants by two streets: **State Street**, which runs north-south, and **Madison Street**, which runs east-west. A street address such as 3523 N. Broadway, is north of Madison Street; a street address such as 2200 W. Belmont, is west of State Street; and so forth for the other directions.

The intersection of State and Madison, which is in the Loop, is also the origination point, or baseline, of house numbers: the

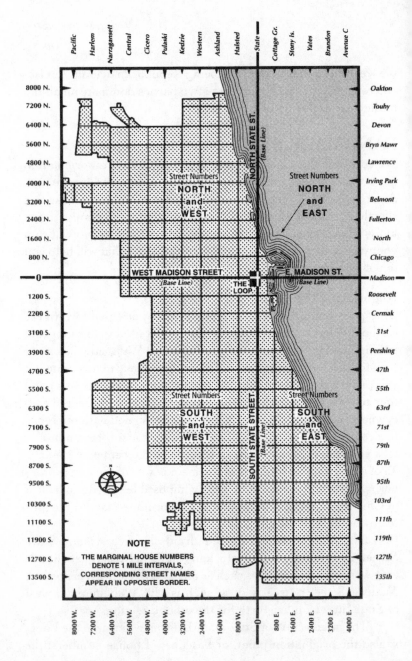

Pacific · Harlem · Narragansett · Central · Cicero · Pulaski · Kedzie · Western · Ashland · Halsted · State · Cottage Gr. · Stony Is. · Yates · Brandon · Avenue C

NORTH STATE ST. (Base Line)

8000 N. — Oakton
7200 N. — Touhy
6400 N. — Devon
5600 N. — Bryn Mawr
4800 N. — Lawrence
4000 N. — Irving Park
3200 N. — Belmont
2400 N. — Fullerton
1600 N. — North
800 N. — Chicago

Street Numbers
NORTH
and
WEST

Street Numbers
NORTH
and
EAST

—0— Madison
WEST MADISON STREET
(Base Line)
E. MADISON ST.
(Base Line)
THE LOOP.

1200 S. — Roosevelt
2200 S. — Cermak
3100 S. — 31st
3900 S. — Pershing
4700 S. — 47th
5500 S. — 55th
6300 S — 63rd
7100 S. — 71st
7900 S. — 79th
8700 S. — 87th
9500 S. — 95th
10300 S. — 103rd
11100 S. — 111th
11900 S. — 119th
12700 S. — 127th
13500 S. — 135th

Street Numbers
SOUTH
and
WEST

Street Numbers
SOUTH
and
EAST

SOUTH STATE STREET (Base Line)

NOTE
THE MARGINAL HOUSE NUMBERS
DENOTE 1 MILE INTERVALS,
CORRESPONDING STREET NAMES
APPEAR IN OPPOSITE BORDER.

8000 W. · 7200 W. · 6400 W. · 5600 W. · 4800 W. · 4000 W. · 3200 W. · 2400 W. · 1600 W. · 800 W. · 0 · 800 E. · 1600 E. · 2400 E. · 3200 E. · 4000 E.

28

first address on State Street (or any other north-south street) north of Madison Street is 1 or 2 N. State Street. By the same token, the first address on Madison Street (or any other east-west street) west of State Street is 1 or 2 W. Madison Street; and so forth for the other directions. The larger the number, the farther away it is from the center. Throughout Chicago, addresses with even numbers are on the north or west side of the street; addresses with odd numbers are on the south or east side of the street.

A street in Chicago has, in theory, 800 house numbers to the mile, though no street actually uses every number. The address of a building then tells you not only which direction it is relative to its base point (State Street or Madison Street), it also tells you how far away it is. On hearing an address like 4624 N. Oakley you know that it's about 5.78 miles (4624 ÷ 800) north of Madison Street; by the same token, 1520 E. 53rd Street is 1.9 miles east of State Street.

If you have followed the explanation so far, you will notice one important shortcoming in this system: an address does *not* tell you where in the city a particular street is located! We know that 4624 N. Oakley is a certain distance north of Madison Street, but we don't know whether it's east or west of State Street, and so without a little more information we can't locate the address in the city precisely. For this, you will need to acquaint yourself with the major streets in Chicago, which are used as guideposts for all the other streets. The system is again very regular and is introduced in some detail in chapter three. Unlike everything else up to now, it requires you to commit to memory some names and numbers. Unless you're a nut for this kind of thing or have to start driving a taxi tomorrow, it's not recommended that you try to learn all this in a day; it will slowly seep in as you make your way around the city.

Opposite: The Chicago House Number Map.

Bronze lions guard the Art Institute on Michigan Avenue. The flags, from left to right, are of the United States, the State of Illinois, Cook County, and the City of Chicago.

Places to Know About

The table below identifies familiar Chicago landmarks. Their location coordinates use the grid system described above: the description 2400 W, 1600 S means 3 miles west, 2 miles south of the intersection of State and Madison streets. Other notable places are located with reference to the two streets that intersect nearest them, or that surround them; this is also common shorthand for describing locations in Chicago.

Landmark/Feature	What is it?	Where is it?
Adler Planetarium	place to see fake stars	Museum Campus
Art Institute	Chicago's foremost collection of serious art	Adams and Michigan
Auditorium Theatre	ornate architectural landmark for dance and music events	Congress and Michigan Ave.

Landmark/Feature	What is it?	Where is it?
Buckingham Fountain	rococco light and water spectacle that circulates 1.5 million gallons of water	in Grant Park, 500 S
Burnham Harbor	harbor for private boats	1300 to 2200 S
Chicago Harbor	harbor for private boats	200 N to 1200 S
Comiskey Park	where Chicago White Sox (baseball) play	35th and Wentworth
Cultural Center	architectural landmark now housing exhibits of general interest	Washington and Michigan Ave.
Daley Plaza	large open space downtown	bounded by Clark, Washington, and Dearborn Streets
De Paul University	private Catholic university	Racine and Armitage
Field Museum of Natural History	Dinosaur bones repository	Museum Campus
Graceland Cemetery	burial place of many prominent Chicagoans	entrance at Grace (3800 N) and Clark
Grant Park	big lakefront park, contains a band shell for outdoor concerts	200 N to 1200 S, along the lake
Greektown	area of Greek restaurants and shops	Halsted and Madison area
International Amphitheater	location for various events, including loud rock concerts	43rd and Halsted
Jackson Park	lakefront park	5600 to 6700 S on the lakefront
John Hancock Center	once the world's tallest building	Michigan Ave. and Walton

31

Landmark/Feature	What is it?	Where is it?
LaSalle Street Station	commuter train station	Congress and LaSalle
Lincoln Park	big lakefront park, contains a zoo	1600 N to 3200 N, along the lake
Loyola University	private Catholic university	6400 N, near the lake
McCormick Place	huge convention complex	2300 S on the lake
Meigs Field	airport for small planes	2200 S on the lake
Merchandise Mart	huge office building	the block bounded by Orleans, Kinzie, Wells, and the Chicago River
Midway Airport	airport for domestic flights	55th and Cicero
Museum Campus	location of three important museums	1200 to 1500 S on the lake
Museum of Science and Industry	just what it sounds like	5700 S on the lake
Navy Pier	lakefront tourist attraction	500 N, projecting into the lake
Northwestern Station	commuter train station downtown	bounded by Washington, Clinton, Madison, and Canal
Northwestern University	top-ranked private university	in Evanston, just north of Chicago
Orchestra Hall	home of the Chicago Symphony Orchestra	Michigan and Adams
Picasso sculpture	huge metal modern art representation of a face	in Daley Plaza
Ravinia	summer home of the Chicago Symphony	Highland Park, a northwest suburb

Landmark/Feature	What is it?	Where is it?
Rosemont Horizon	place for concerts, sports, and other events	Rosemont, a northwest suburb
Sears Tower	tallest building in North America	bounded by Wacker, Jackson, Franklin, and Adams
Shedd Aquarium	exotic fish hotel	Museum Campus
Soldier Field	where Chicago Bears (football) and Chicago Fire (soccer) play	1500 S on the lake
Symphony Center	new name for Orchestra Hall	Michigan Ave. and Adams
Thompson Center	State of Illinois office building	downtown, bounded by Randolph, LaSalle, Lake, and Clark
Traffic Court	where you go to fight or pay a parking ticket	321 N. LaSalle
Union Station	Amtrak (national) and commuter train station	downtown, bounded by Adams, Clinton, Jackson, and Canal
United Center	where Chicago Bulls (basketball) and Chicago Blackhawks (hockey) play	Ashland and Madison
University of Chicago	top-ranked private university	in Hyde Park, on the South Side
University of Illinois at Chicago	Chicago campus of Illinois' biggest and best state school	W. of Halsted between Harrison and Cermak Road
Wrigley Field	where Chicago Cubs (baseball) play	Addison and Clark
Wrigley Building	landmark terracotta-faced office building	410 N. Michigan

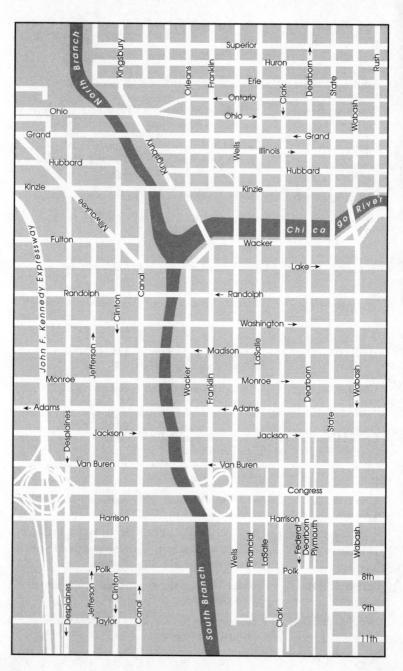

34   *Downtown Chicago*

CHAPTER TWO

BEHIND THE FAÇADE

*Chicago — is — oh well, a façade of skyscrapers facing a lake,
and behind the façade every type of dubiousness.*
—E.M. Forster, *Letters*

The big question facing the new arrival in Chicago is not much different from the one faced by any foreigner new to urban America: what really is going on here? Paradoxically, the experience of culture shock for foreigners in the United States is often quite acute. American culture may be the most exported and in many ways the best known in the world, but the reality of American life is very different from its widely distributed tokens. Popular depictions of American life in movies, music, and advertising probably contrast as sharply with the reality as a science fiction novel does with a real trip into outer space: until you are there and can experience the place through all of your senses, you can hardly imagine what it is really like. Most things you have heard or read about the United States may have given you expectations that stand in the way of experiencing the place for what it is. This chapter will not attempt to disabuse you of any notions you may have about American culture, or particularly about life in Chicago; the hands-on experience of the place will accomplish that. But we will look at some of the things you can expect to experience in Chicago, while trying to paint an accurate picture of Chicagoans that may go some way toward explaining why they are the way they are.

ETHNIC DEMOGRAPHICS

In one sense all big American cities look and feel alike: skyscrapers and traffic are concentrated downtown, the same stores and restaurants seem to be found everywhere owing to the success of franchising, and people dress more or less the same wherever you go, with seasonal variations. What then makes Chicago different? Why are 8 million people here instead of somewhere else?

Chicago today is a multicultural and multiracial city similar to nearly all cities in the Western world. It is not as cosmopolitan as many coastal cities and many national capitals, but it still boasts a wide spectrum of national enclaves. A hundred years ago, Chicago was in many senses more cosmopolitan than it is today. Then, 75 percent of Chicagoans were either foreign-born or first generation Americans; today it is closer to 20 percent. A breakdown of immigration patterns will bring today's picture into sharper relief.

The foundation of Chicago's early immigrant community was German. At the turn of the 20th century, Germans made up just over 25 percent of the population, as much as the next three identifiable ethnic groups combined (Irish, Poles, and Swedes, in that order). So dominant was the German ethnic group that many advertisements, especially for jobs and houses, appeared in both

English and German. By the middle of the century the numbers were different. Foreign immigration had dwindled to nearly insignificant levels and immigrants and first-generation Chicagoans represented less than 45 percent of the population. Poles had become the dominant European ethnic group, followed by Germans, Italians, Czechs (Bohemians, as they were then called), and Irish. The largest identifiable ethnic group was African-Americans, who made up more than 13 percent of the population, a result of migration from the South after the end of World War II.

Ethnicity in Chicago today is more diverse but less pronounced for any single group than it was in the 20th century, with one exception: Latinos, or Hispanics as they are also called. Absent at the turn of the century and comprising less than 1 percent of the population in 1950, Latinos today are the largest identified ethnic group in Chicagoland, making up nearly a quarter of the population, though it must be said that this is partly because the label "Latino" groups many diverse nationalities; Mexicans, Cubans, and Puerto Ricans are the main ones.

In broader strokes, Chicago today (or more properly Chicagoland, since the figures take in all of the metropolitan area) is 72 percent white, 19 percent black, and less than 0.5 percent each of Native American and Asian. A majority of Chicagoland residents still identify themselves with their ethnic origin. After the Latinos, Germans remain the biggest group, followed by Irish, Poles, Italians, Czechs, English, Swedes, and Russians. Of today's Chicagoans, 65 percent were born in Chicagoland, 9 percent elsewhere in the Midwest, 5 percent elsewhere in the United States, and only 11 percent were foreign-born.

It is perhaps ironic that people descended from the largest single European ethnic strain in Chicago today are the group that is least likely to be identified as an ethnic group: the Germans. This is partly because those of German stock have integrated themselves into the fabric of Chicago so thoroughly as to lose a sense of separateness. Another significant factor in the "erasing" of German heritage was the effect of two World Wars, both of which made it inadvisable to be obviously German or to extol German culture. As a result of the wars, German language virtually disappeared from use in Chicago by mid-century. Other European groups maintain a more visible ethnic identity, especially the Poles (Chicago has more Poles than any other city except Warsaw) and to a lesser extent the Irish and Italians.

A lawyer's office in Logan Square, catering to the Polish- and Spanish-speaking communities.

Chicagoland today is still a primary destination for immigrants to the United States. Among American cities it ranks fourth (after New York, Los Angeles, and Miami) as a destination for immigrants, with the majority of arrivals (four in five) coming from Mexico, Poland, and India, in that order. The most recent statistics available show that about 40,000 foreigners obtain legal residence in Chicagoland each year. The majority of newcomers today join family members who are already here and who came in the previous generation or perhaps only a few years ago. Chicago remains the cultural and ethnic melange that it has been historically, with slightly different ingredients.

RELIGION AND SPIRITUALITY

Some form of Christianity, even if it is only rudimentary beliefs, holds a place in the spiritual life of most Chicagoans. Christian values, even if not openly professed, underlie much of civil life and manners. A belief in God, even if a very naive and unexamined one, is the rule rather than the exception for Chicagoans, as it is for most Americans. But this is considerably less true than it was 50 years ago, as more and more people embrace a religion they have found, or no religion at all, rather than the one they grew up with.

In concert with the American way of accentuating the personality and the individual, religion (so-called) may be experienced and practiced by Chicagoans not so much as a spiritual path but as a public statement about who they are, or a compatible accessory of their lifestyle. This is not to suggest that genuine spiritual growth, development, and experience, together with an integrated system of morality that guides personal choice, is absent from the life of Chicagoans. Rather it means that you should not be surprised to discover that these noble and traditional components of religious life are not necessarily what is offered by the organized and most visible religious bodies in Chicagoland. They

39

are dependent for support on the public and have adapted with the times to give the people what they want.

Many cultures and countries with a majority of people who adhere to one religion hold that religion as a rallying point, a place for common ground among all the people. This is not the case with Christianity in the United States, despite the fact that so many Americans profess to be Christians. There has been a tendency from the beginning in America to separate religion from other aspects of life, especially from government, and that tendency continues today. Religion is something that people often pursue in their leisure time, but most Americans feel that it is not something you should bring with you to work or school. People who proselytize or even speak openly about their beliefs or religious experiences often get a frosty reception—though this does not stop them.

Because of the large number of different Christian sects and denominations, and because the Bible is subject to so many differing interpretations, there are greater and more visible divisions within Christianity than between Christianity and other religions practiced in Chicago. The biggest division today is between what many people call the "religious right"—fundamentalist Christian sects that actively oppose abortion and homosexuality, among other targets—and more liberal and tolerant forms of Christianity that emphasize the Bible's teachings of love and tolerance, rather than using it as a sort of battering weapon.

The old ethnic groups in Chicago were primarily Europeans from Catholic countries, and today Catholics outnumber Protestants in the Chicago area about two to one. There are fewer Catholic than Protestant churches, but the Catholic churches are bigger. The Protestant scene is dominated by Lutherans (the German influence), but there are significant numbers of other mainline Protestant denominations, such as Methodists, Presbyterians, and Anglicans, who are called Episcopalians in the United States.

Baptist congregations have a strong following in black communities where "storefront" churches—those without a purpose-built sanctuary, usually under the leadership of charismatic and emotional evangelists—are also popular.

Muslims, Eastern Orthodox Christians, Jews of all expressions, and Buddhists representing all the various schools are all present in Chicagoland—at least 100,000 of each. Chicago is the world headquarters of the Black Muslims, officially called the Nation of Islam, a Western adaptation of Islam with a very strong following in Chicago's black community. Immigrant Muslims from the subcontinent and the Middle East largely eschew this Western version of their religion and build their own mosques in areas where their populations are concentrated.

LANGUAGE

American English is the predominant language of Chicago but there are pockets in the city where other languages will serve you much better than English. The main contender is Spanish, which is well enough established to be considered a semiofficial second language. Many public notices appear in Spanish and English, and Spanish-language advertising is common on billboards in some areas of the city, as well as on public transportation. Other areas of the city with ethnic groups that use their own language are:

- the Northwest side along Milwaukee Avenue, where Polish will serve you better than English
- Chinatown and Argyle Street (5000 N), where Chinese (and to a lesser extent, Vietnamese on Argyle Street) does the job
- Pockets of Devon Avenue and in Evanston, where Russian is gaining a foothold

The English spoken in Chicago is very standard as American English goes; people in the Midwest speak with an accent that most people around the world would readily identify as an American accent. A small and probably disappearing variety of

41

A shop on Argyle Street catering to the Chinese and Vietnamese.

speech that might be called a Chicago accent can still be heard in some white working-class areas of the city, such as the Southwest Side. Its most identifiable characteristic is the substitution of ∂ for the *th* sound in words such as "this" and "that." The late mayor Richard J. Daley was a natural with the native Chicago accent; his son, the current mayor, shows faint vestiges of it.

Nearly everything that has reached American shores from the Old World undergoes a transformation and words are no exception. Thus if you are familiar with any European languages you may find the pronunciation of some Chicagoland streets and place names quaint. Words of French origin suffer the worst insults. Here is a short guide that will enable you to adopt the local pronunciation and thus avoid being spotted immediately as a "dumb foreigner."

Name	What is it?	Pronunciation
Belmont	street in Chicago, 3200 N	BEL-mont
Calumet	lake in south Chicago	cal-ye-MET
Des Plaines	northwest Chicago suburb	dez PLAINZ
Devon	street in Chicago, 6400 N	de-VONN
Diversey	street in Chicago, 2800 N	de-VER-si
Goethe	street in Chicago, 1300 N	GO-thi
Montrose	street in Chicago, 4400 N	MON-troz
Touhy	street in Chicago, 7200 N	TOO-ee
Vincennes	diagonal street in south Chicago	vin-SENZ

ROLES OF MEN AND WOMEN

People who know Americans only through their representation in television and movies are very likely to have a bizarre notion of what relations between the sexes are really like. You have to remember that in the absence of knowing Americans on a day-to-day, mundane basis, you may well have absorbed information about their behavior toward each other through the prism of your own culture, which distorts the picture to some degree; and if the picture came from movies and television, it was probably not too accurate in the first place. So for a few moments, forget everything you think you know or may have heard about men and women in American cities. Here are a few points about the modern urban American man and woman that might help you to understand them better.

The word that is supposed to define and direct relations between American men and women today is *equality*. This causes ongoing but not necessarily problematic tension, because relations are not on an equal basis in many situations and probably never will be in some. In all situations in which a law of any kind applies, equality is supposed to be the rule: women are supposed to be granted the same rights, opportunities, and protection as men in employment and education, for example. But women are not routinely treated equally; they often have to assert themselves to keep from being discriminated against, especially in the workplace.

While women expect equal treatment under the law, both men and women are comfortable with a more traditional assignment of roles that leaves some room for chivalry, good manners, and recognition of men as protectors of women. Men still (though much less frequently than in the past) open doors for women, and (with even *less* frequency) yield a seat to them on public transportation, especially to an older, pregnant, or heavily laden woman. But it is not out of place for a woman to do these same things for a man when there is a reason for it.

In matters concerning romance, men still take a more active role than women, in that they more typically initiate, plan, and pay for "dates," or romantic outings for two people. But it is important to be aware that relations between men and women in American cities are *very* open and friendly in comparison with standards that prevail in most parts of the world. It is possible and common for men and women to socialize without there being any suggestion of greater intimacy between them. And it is possible for them to be intimate without any implication that they are making some kind of lifelong commitment to each other. These patterns can prove a stumbling block for men from more traditional cultures, who may think that an American woman is "coming on" to them, or indicating her availability for romance, when in fact she is just being friendly and enjoying herself, and not making any kind of statement about romance whatever.

By the same token, women coming to Chicagoland from cultures where they traditionally take a subservient, submissive, or passive role may experience difficulties adjusting to American expectations of them. Here you are expected to stand up for yourself and have your own opinions about everything. There may be a temptation to perceive American men and women as brash, aggressive, and even rude, but by American standards they are probably none of these, they are simply treating you as they treat everyone, as an *equal.*

There is probably no single area of human relations where rules are less transportable between cultures than in the area of relations between the sexes. The upshot of this is that you can't really assume that you know what's going on between men and women in Chicago based on their behavior toward each other. And you may not have, at least at first, a very good idea of what their intentions are toward you. To the extent that you are able then, it pays to take a backseat initially, observe what you can, and find a confidante of the same sex if possible who can shed light on any confusions that may arise for you about what men and women are doing.

Men and Men, Women and Women

As a complicating factor in this sensitive area, gay people are increasingly accepted in most areas of modern urban life on an equal footing with "straight" people. You are very likely to meet with openly gay people where you work or study, and you may meet same-sex couples at parties or through other friends of yours. It is also common for gay men to have as their good friends straight women (single or married), though it is rare for gay women to associate much on a friendly basis with straight men.

These arrangements fly in the face of established decorum in most parts of the world, and indeed in many parts of the United States. American cities are a magnet for gay people who seek acceptance that they cannot find in smaller towns and rural areas, which are a great deal more conservative and traditional. Chicago is the biggest city between the coasts so it has a large, active, and very visible gay population. City government has traditionally been very cooperative with the gay community, and many candidates for public office have openly courted the gay vote, recognizing that it is very influential in many parts of the city.

STAGES OF LIFE

Urban Americans progress through the same stages of life recognized everywhere, but may give them different emphasis, owing to demographic patterns and cultural values. If there is a uniquely American pattern in the progress from cradle to grave, it is probably the extent to which institutions outside the family are involved in the development and care of the individual, and the ongoing emphasis on individuality and self-improvement that begins in early childhood and never stops.

Babies and young children hold the same special place in the hearts of Chicagoans that they do the world over. The fact that Americans often wait until they are well into their thirties before having children, and the fact that they may turn the children over to the care of professionals while they are still in diapers (because both parents work), could lead you to think that parenthood is just a kind of sideline. You will see with experience of Americans that it is not. Chicagoans are as emotionally invested in their children as parents everywhere. Because children are held to be so precious and because in large cities there is no sense of community that unites people not already known to each other, you may notice a tendency for parents to be overprotective of their children and suspicious of any stranger's interaction with them. Behavior toward other people's children that in your own culture would be seen as friendly, innocent, or well-intentioned may be perceived as threatening or suspect here. For that reason, it is probably good advice not to intervene in the affairs of children who don't belong to you in any way, unless invited to do so by a parent.

With the onset of adolescence, a fully-fledged type emerges. The American teenager is the focus of numerous sociological studies, millions of dollars in advertising, and untold hours of angst on the part of parents who wonder whatever happened to their little darlings. The teenage years are normally seen as years of rebellion on the part of youngsters, and of challenge on the part of parents who have to deal with their children's growing autonomy and exposure to the temptations of sex and drugs. Parents from other cultures must be ready to face challenges about raising teenagers in America that were probably not part of the picture at home.

Generational Types

There are at present three generational groups of adults in America that are recognized as units of a sort. The term **Generation X** refers to people born after 1965, perhaps up to 1980 or so, who are now young adults. This generation grew up in an era of diminished expectations and may in many cases end up being less well-off economically than their parents, or so we are told. Look around and judge for yourself! The generation ahead of them are the **baby boomers**, the biggest demographic bulge in the United States, who were born between 1946 and 1958, although the cutoff is never quite distinct. Baby boomers, who are now in their 40s to mid-50s, have the most economic and political influence of any identifiable group and are viewed as the group for whose convenience everything is organized. As this group ages and enters retirement, it is expected to be their needs that drive economic policy in many important respects.

People over the age of about 60 are called **seniors**, or **senior citizens**. They are afforded many economic concessions by various businesses, in housing, in medical care, and on public transportation, but in general they are not afforded the respect that comes naturally with old age in many cultures. Elderly people who are no longer able to take care of themselves independently may live in an "assisted living" facility, where some of their daily needs are taken care of by visiting professionals, or they may be moved to nursing homes. It is usually not the rule for people to care for elderly parents at home, though it is still fairly common in ethnic and immigrant communities.

Got a Problem? See a Professional!

Americans move around a great deal in their lives and many eventually migrate to cities, where jobs, especially for educated people, are concentrated. This often means that people live quite a distance from members of their immediate family, who in many other cultures normally provide the individual's primary support network. A phenomenon related to this—as well as to the high degree of individuality, personal independence, and personal freedom among urban Americans—is the relatively large number of people who participate in some kind of therapy or self-help program. Since so many urban Americans undergo psychotherapy or some other kind of therapy at some point in their adult lives, there is very little stigma attached to doing so. Many people talk about their experiences in therapy openly; it is often seen as a positive step that a person is taking to try to improve his or her life. A less openly talked about aspect of the therapeutic experience, but one that is fairly common, is the use of prescription drugs to treat depression, anxiety, sleep disorders, and other ailments that seem to go hand-in-hand with modern city life.

A surprising number of children and adolescents may also receive counseling from professionals outside the family at some point, especially if they are having difficulties in school or if they cause disruption there. A whole industry exists now to maintain children on prescription drugs of various kinds that are supposed to make them more socially cohesive.

A more community-based approach to dealing with personal problems is a **recovery program**, sometimes called a **12-step program**. These programs, mostly modeled on Alcoholics Anonymous, start from the premise that individuals, try as they might, are unable to willfully free themselves from addictive, self-destructive behavior of various sorts, such as overeating, drinking too much, dependence on drugs, dependence on sex, and the like. The programs guide people to better self-understanding through spirituality. People participating in the programs attend frequent meetings, typically held in church community rooms, and talk about their problems and progress in dealing with them. There is a whole dialect unique to these programs that is foreign to anyone who does not participate, but some of its terms are creeping into the mainstream, such as *being in denial, codependency, higher power,* and *recovery.* The premises and methods of these programs are deeply rooted in American culture and may be confusing and off-putting to someone coming from abroad, but on the other hand, they are surefire ways to meet people!

THE PLACE OF RACE AND CLASS

Historically Chicago has been one of the most racially divided cities in the United States, a country that is full of racially divided cities. The problem has not gone away, though it can confidently be said that racial divisions are less important and prominent today than they have been at any time in the past. "White flight" — a phenomenon that began nearly half a century ago when white people left neighborhoods that blacks were moving into — has slowed to its lowest level in decades. Neighborhoods that are experiencing the greatest racial change now are those where middle-class whites leave to be replaced by middle-class blacks. Those interested in the details of racial politics in Chicago can find dozens of book-length treatments. The concern here is only to give a picture of how Chicagoans generally perceive race today and how that might affect you if you are a member of a group that has traditionally been identified as a minority race.

Institutionalized racism—where the policies and practices of institutions are actually based on preferential treatment of some people according to their race—does not officially exist anymore, and numerous laws are in place to insure that it doesn't. But institutions are the product of history and the people who perpetuate them, and so this means that *de facto* racism survives in institutions dominated by people whose minds are rooted in the past. Your encounter with issues of race will nearly always be at the individual, face-to-face level, but this individual may be representing an institution.

How might you be perceived? The biggest, and rather crude boxes that Chicagoans are likely to sort people in, based on appearances and speech, are

- black—people of sub-Saharan African descent
- Latino—people whose first language is Spanish, and whose ancestry is from one of the Spanish-speaking countries or areas of the New World, which in Chicago usually means Mexicans, Cubans, Puerto Ricans, and Central Americans. Note that people from Spain are normally thought of as Europeans, not as Latinos.
- Asian—Chinese, Japanese, Southeast Asian, and Korean people
- Middle Eastern—people from the Arabian peninsula, North Africa, and the eastern Mediterranean. The less-informed term for these is "Arab."
- Indians—people who appear to be from the subcontinent, that is, from India, Pakistan, or Bangladesh

People who don't fall into one of these appearance-based categories and who do not have dark skin fall into the value-free category of "white."

The Sears Tower is framed in the distance by buildings in Chinatown on the near South Side.

For some people these categories are just for convenience and do not carry any prejudicial associations; others may have well-defined but probably inaccurate stereotypes to go with each sort of person. A few people, especially those less educated or in some way disadvantaged, may perceive any individual only through the distorting and negative prism of prejudicial attitudes based on category. You will meet Americans that exhibit each of these characteristics.

The experience of black Americans, now often called African-Americans, and their place in urban American society cannot go unremarked because this group is still such a long way from attaining equality. Many laws and programs exist to aid American blacks and ensure that they don't suffer discrimination, but in fact they are still highly discriminated against in many quarters. People of black African descent from other parts of the world who settle in Chicago are often confused and bewildered by the treatment they receive, especially if they come from a country with a black majority population, or a country where blacks enjoy equality with other identified racial groups. It has to be understood that the legacy of slavery and the premise of racial inferiority that enabled it to exist will require many more generations to reach its end in the United States. Slavery flourished in North America for more than 300 years; it was abolished just over 100 years ago.

Class is a matter far more subtle and ambiguous in American society than the matter of race. There are those who argue Americans have no class system at all, while others insist that American culture is riddled with class distinctions. We will not intervene deeply in the dispute but only make a few observations. First of all, money talks in America. Making money is a sign of success, and economic success opens just about any apparently closed door. In effect, a person's background does not limit his or her potential to rise within the socioeconomic system; only his or her abilities impose any limits. Secondly, the uniform education system across the United States means that practically everyone, except the minorities who are very poor or very rich, shares a similar cultural background; they all grow up studying similar books, watching the same television programs, and engaging in many of the same activities. This tends to minimize class distinctions within the broad mainstream that thinks of itself as middle-class. Thirdly, Americans have always been self-reliant do-it-yourselfers. Apart from the very exceptional case of slavery, there has never existed a servant underclass in the United States. As a result, Americans don't know any of the many behaviors that exist in other cultures for "keeping people in their place." This is why Americans are apt to be familiar and friendly with all the people they deal with and to treat everyone as an equal: the manner you assume with your barber needn't be any different from the one you assume with your stockbroker.

The upshot of all this is that class is not a subject that occupies urban Americans very much, or that enters much into their conversation. People who find the most to say about class distinctions among Americans are usually those who have developed their awareness of it somewhere else, in a culture where it is considerably more prominent.

CRACKING THE AMERICAN NUT

So far we have painted a broad picture of Chicagoans, but there is still the tougher question: why do these people act the way they do and say the things they say? You will very likely spend a lot of your early time in Chicago trying to deconstruct the behavior of your new American friends and colleagues and search for hidden meanings in what they say and do. This can be a profitable activity if you know a few of their rules and values, but if you try to interpret Chicagoans' behavior according to the rules of your own culture, you could very well end up way off the track. We will therefore conclude this chapter by trying to give some shape to the psyche of the typical Midwestern urban American, with the proviso that this is also necessarily a very broad picture and cannot attempt to explain a given individual. At best it can provide you with a few tools to help you understand what motivates the natives. The observations are organized around common American idioms that tell us a lot about the way Americans think.

Tell It Like It Is

To a degree that people from many parts of the world find shocking and confusing, Americans like to be direct. "Tell it like it is" means just say what you mean without adding or subtracting anything; don't try to give an appearance of something that is not true. Another idiom with similar meaning is "be straight." When you are straight with someone you tell them exactly what's going on, without trying to be subtle, devious, or deceptive. Being straight and telling it like it is are both admirable things in the American system of values. This does not mean that people don't tell lies or try to communicate something indirectly, but you should know from the outset that a lot of attempts at subtlety with Americans will be a complete waste of time. They won't have a clue what you're trying to communicate. You will find relations much easier if you do it the American way—just say what you mean.

By the same token, you will have to develop a tolerance for being dealt with directly: being told in a few words, for example, that some work you have done is not quite what was wanted, or being given a simple "no" to a suggestion of yours for which you might have expected more discussion. No rudeness is intended; this is just the American way.

Get Things Done

Another idiom that crops up in many areas of American life is the phrase "get things done." It means to accomplish things, to finish things that you have started. Someone who has a "get-things-done attitude" is viewed positively as a person of action, a person who can be successful. Americans don't like settling for a situation that is less than satisfactory, and they don't like "muddling through," even though life requires us to do so frequently. A problem to an American is something that requires a solution, not something to be tolerated. So you shouldn't be surprised at the impatience Americans may express about something that you find perfectly tolerable or would simply choose to ignore until it goes away. The American approach lies more on the side of doing something about it, rather than letting it do something to you!

Pick Yourself Up By The Bootstraps

Consistent with the previous points is the idea that your success depends, to a large degree, on your own efforts. Americans like to think, and in many respects it is probably true, that any American child could grow up to be president of the United States. It is undeniable that an individual's success or failure in life is influenced by a great number of factors beyond the individual's control, but the American tendency is to give little attention to these matters (since there is nothing you can do about them anyway) and to focus on what you *can* do. An implication of this view is that the individual is the creator of his own condition. This gives rise to the social mobility that we already noted: there is nothing to hold the individual back from attaining much more status, wealth, education, and the like than his or her parents had. It is not at all unusual to find people at the top of their professions who come from very humble origins. You will be surprised at the number of such people who are the children or grandchildren of immigrants. They prove a cherished belief among Americans that anybody can be successful if they set their mind to it.

You may also occasionally meet people who have squandered the advantages they were born with and who are living a life considerably less comfortable than the one enjoyed by their parents or siblings. While many external factors may contribute to this phenomenon as well, the popular American view is that people

55

simply make the wrong choices—in their marriage for example or in their failure to apply themselves—and so fail of their own accord. Americans don't necessarily feel a duty to "rescue" a member of their family who has fallen on hard times.

Viewing the world this way wouldn't last long without an inherent optimism, and that is also very much a feature of American thinking. People like to believe, and very often say, that things will work out for the best. A Hollywood movie that doesn't have a happy, even a triumphant, ending runs a serious risk of being a box-office flop, because Americans like happy endings.

Let It All Hang Out

American English has a popular idiom that says "let it all hang out," which loosely means "be completely free, natural, and uninhibited; express whatever you have to express." While such a notion might strike terror in the hearts of people from gentler cultures, letting it all hang out, in most contexts, is something that most Americans would view as a positive or admirable thing. This points to a central tenet in American culture: personal freedom and individuality have intrinsic value, and you have a responsibility to "be somebody," to cultivate your own personal likes and dislikes in order to distinguish yourself from others.

There is certainly scope in a larger analysis to talk about whether this is a good thing or not, but that is not our purpose here. We simply want to note that this is a fact about modern Americans that helps explain their behavior in many situations. You may wonder why a perfect stranger, such as somebody on a bus or a cashier in a store, takes an opportunity to tell you something idiosyncratic about themselves, or it may seem odd to you that a Chicagoan you know would decline a social opportunity with you in order to go and work out at the gym. Both of these are symptoms of people cultivating and expressing individuality, activities that Americans find, or at least think that they will find, fulfilling.

A corollary of American individualism is that Americans you meet may often have a need to be alone. It is very common for unmarried people to live alone and to spend a great deal of time alone. If you come from a culture that places more value on companionship and cultivating interpersonal relationships, you may have to check a tendency in yourself to rescue an American from spending time alone. Unless you have a lot of evidence to the contrary, chances are that Americans you know are spending time alone because they like to. The "one-person household" constitutes nearly a third of all households in Chicago.

Strut Your Stuff

The idiom "strut your stuff" means to show off what you do well, to demonstrate your (hopefully unique) abilities in some way. It perhaps epitomizes more than all others the fondness of Americans — some would even call it compulsion — to distinguish themselves from others, to stand out from the crowd for some achievement or characteristic, however small. Foreigners often remark on the tireless ability of Americans to talk about themselves and the minutiae of their personal experiences, especially regarding their likes and dislikes, comforts and discomforts, or victories and defeats. From the perspective of another culture this often appears as loud, crass, and boorish, and it is the thing that so easily distinguishes groups of Americans when they are abroad. It is a challenge to try to understand this sort of behavior within the context of American culture, where it is not remarkable, or calculated to achieve some effect: it is just normal. Everybody has to be somebody, and the way to do it is to speak and behave in a way that illustrates your uniqueness.

CHAPTER THREE

CHICAGO ON THE GROUND

When we were in space we saw Chicago. It is a very big city
with many avenues, many streets, and a lot of big buildings.
But Chicago on the ground is much better than from space.
—Alexei Leonov, Soviet cosmonaut, 1975

In the most recently published *Places Rated Almanac*, which compares the amenities of the metropolitan centers in the United States, Chicago ranks number one in the transportation category: easiest to get in and out of, and easiest to move around in. It is the country's center for air passenger and freight traffic, the hub of America's passenger railroad system, and also the most centrally located major city in North America. This chapter will acquaint you with all means of motion and locomotion within, into, and out of the city.

Chicago's Airports

Chicago's two busy airports, O'Hare (airline routing code ORD) and Midway (MDW), have direct service to 280 destinations and are served by more than 3,300 flights every day. In terms of passenger volume, O'Hare is the busiest airport in the world with an annual load of nearly 80 million passengers. A current political hot potato is the possibility of a third major airport to be built that would serve the Chicago area, but even if approved, it is years away from completion.

Both Chicago airports have convenient public transportation links to the downtown area and both are located near expressways that allow quick access by car as well—provided that you don't get caught in a traffic jam, which is actually a pretty common experience on the way to or from both airports. Only O'Hare (located northwest of the city) handles international air traffic. You should allow yourself a full hour to reach either airport from the Loop, though in many cases you will get there in less time. If you're taking a taxi, the travel time to either airport can be from 20 minutes to an hour, depending on the traffic.

O'Hare offers direct flights to several American, European, and Asian cities, and good connections to anywhere in the world, as well as within North America. It is a hub for United Airlines, one of the biggest U.S. carriers. Bargain flights to various U.S. and North American cities are more common from Midway (on the southwest side of the city) than out of O'Hare.

If you arrive at the international terminal at O'Hare there are free luggage carts available. If you are flying into O'Hare on a domestic flight or into Midway, luggage carts are available only for rental from machines that require you to deposit money in them; so be sure you have some U.S. currency in your pocket. O'Hare Airport is completely accessible to the handicapped; you can always avoid the use of stairs or escalators by taking an elevator. Midway is a more old-fashioned, ground-based airport that

A rainy afternoon at Midway Airport.

has steps from the ground level to the jetway at every gate, but it is currently undergoing a major modernization and expansion program.

Meigs Field, a small lakefront airport for mostly private jets, planes, and helicopters, is located just north of McCormick Place and south of the Adler Planetarium. It is certainly the best place to land if you're coming in your own plane!

Travel by Train

Aside from commuter trains (discussed below), Chicago is served by several passenger trains, and is the rail hub of North America for both passenger and freight trains. All interstate train travel in the United States is regulated by **Amtrak**, a government-chartered company. Because of the size of the country and the time required to travel from one place to another overland, air travel has come to be preferred to train travel in the United States during the past 40 years or so, with the result that railroads are not nearly as well developed or modern as in many other parts of the world. Trains are quite slow compared to European or Japanese trains, and serve a relatively small number of cities, which seem to be ever decreasing in number. Over most routes the cost of a train ticket—traditionally a factor that makes trains attractive—is not necessarily cheaper than a plane ticket to the same destination if you take the trouble to shop around for low air fares. So the end result is that not so many people travel by train, and those who try it for the first time may never go back.

Disadvantages notwithstanding, America's railroads pass through some very scenic countryside, and there is direct service from Chicago to most major American cities on the West Coast, East Coast, and Gulf Coast. All trains leave from and arrive at Union Station. You can pick up schedules, maps, and fare information at the station, or visit Amtrak's website at **www.amtrak. com** to take an armchair tour of the U.S. passenger rail system.

Intercity and Interstate Buses
Numerous regional and national bus lines serve Chicago. Greyhound is the main company and operates a terminal at 630 W. Harrison Street, just southwest of the Loop. The nearest subway stop is Clinton, on the Blue Line. There is also bus service from O'Hare Airport to a few cities elsewhere in Illinois and in Wisconsin. Bus travel is the most economical of all long-distance travel, but also the slowest. The unsavory atmosphere that prevails at bus terminals in Chicago and elsewhere probably keeps many people away who might otherwise travel by bus.

GETTING AROUND IN CHICAGOLAND
Before we look at the various means for moving around on, under, or above the ground in Chicagoland, a quick revisit to the plan of the city is in order. As mentioned in chapter 1, if you can

master the details of the house numbering system you will never get lost: the street signs in combination with house numbers tell you where you are in the city in relation to the Loop. We learned earlier that the city is divided into quadrants defined by State Street and Madison Street. These two streets intersect in the Loop. Addresses north of Madison Street are prefixed by N, those south of Madison Street by S, and similarly for addresses east and west of State Street. House numbering begins with number 1 at State and Madison and numbers increase as distance from the center increases. There are 800 house numbers to the mile, so an address such as 4400 S. Kedzie is 5.5 miles south of Madison Street.

The general plan of the city is that every mile there is a major through street, called a thoroughfare, used by nonlocal traffic. The major streets always allow for two-way traffic, and some of them have two lanes in each direction. By contrast, the streets in-between the major streets may be one-way or discontinuous. On the west side, the north-south thoroughfares are Halsted Street (800 W), Ashland Avenue (1600 W), Western Avenue (2400 W), and so forth; on the north side, the thoroughfares are Chicago Avenue (800 N), North Avenue (1600 N), Fullerton Avenue (2400 N), and so forth. North-south thoroughfares east of State Street (all of these are on the South Side) also follow this pattern. The streets at half-mile intervals (e.g. Division Street 1200 N, Racine Avenue 1200 W) can be thought of as semithoroughfares and are often designed to carry as much traffic as the one-mile interval thoroughfares.

On the South Side of the city, the east-west thoroughfares carry numbers instead of names. The streets are not multiples of 400, but they are at the same intervals. For slight irregularities in numbers to the mile on the South Side, see the map on page 28.

Thoroughfares are landmarks for all Chicagoans and are used to locate other smaller streets that fall between them. Ask somebody where Barry Avenue (3100 N) is, and they'll likely tell you it's between Belmont and Diversey. For that reason it will benefit you to memorize — either as a conscious exercise or by the easier but slower method of osmosis — the names of main thorough-fares and their locations. This will make it easy to find your way around the city, and to understand directions given to you.

You will notice that street signs are small horizontal green signs affixed to light poles at intersections. Pay no attention to the brown signs, which give the "honorary" names of various streets. These names don't appear on maps and are not known beyond the neighborhoods where they are found; people don't refer to them when giving directions.

Exceptions to the Grid

Superimposed on the regular grid of Chicago streets are a few diagonal streets and expressways that cut through the regular pattern and allow faster travel if you're headed in a direction other than strictly north, south, east, or west.

Street	Located
Clark Street	200 W in the loop; veers to the NW at Diversey and continues out of the city
Lincoln Avenue	Starts at 1800 N and LaSalle Street; heads NW
Clybourn Avenue	Starts at Division and Orleans; heads NW to Belmont and Western
Elston Avenue	Starts at Chicago and Milwaukee; heads NW to Peterson and Milwaukee
Milwaukee Avenue	Starts at Lake and Canal; heads NW out of the city
Grand Avenue	400 N to Western Ave; then veers to the NW
Ogden Avenue	Starts near North and Halsted; heads SW out of the city
Archer Avenue	Starts near 18th and State; heads SW out of the city

Expressways in Chicago—what you may call a motorway or freeway—carry fast traffic, except of course when they are jammed with cars. These roads are normally referred to by their names, but they also carry numbers as part of the Interstate or U.S. highway system. The following table identifies the expressways. Studying the names while looking at a map will make sense of the scheme a lot faster:

Name	Number	Location
Stevenson Expressway	I-55	Runs SW from 23rd Street and Lake Shore Drive
Chicago Skyway (toll road)	I-90	Branches from the Dan Ryan Expressway at 65th Street and heads SE toward Indiana
Eisenhower Expressway	I-90	Runs W from the Loop to the western suburbs
Kennedy Expressway	I-90	Runs NW from the Loop to O'Hare Airport
Calumet Expressway	I-94	Continuation of the Dan Ryan, going farther S and E
Dan Ryan Expressway	I-94	Runs S from the Loop to 95 Street
Edens Expressway	I-94	Branches from the Kennedy Expressway at Irving Park Road and heads N
Lake Shore Drive	US 41	Parallels the lakefront throughout the city

The street system may have a logic but it is still useful to have a detailed street map of Chicagoland. Maps are widely available in bookstores and gas stations. A popular and very detailed map is published by the *Chicago Tribune* newspaper. There is also a useful street guide in the front of the Chicago telephone directory (Yellow Pages) that locates all streets with reference to the house numbering system and equates them with post office ZIP codes.

PUBLIC TRANSPORTATION

Three authorities control public transportation in Chicagoland: the Chicago Transit Authority (CTA), principally responsible for buses, subways, and elevated trains (Ls) within the city limits; Metra, which operates commuter trains between Chicago and suburbs of the six-county northeastern Illinois area (including northwest Indiana); and Pace, which does what Metra does, only with buses rather than trains. If you live within the Chicago city limits you will probably deal mostly with the CTA; if you live in the suburbs, you will use Metra or Pace-operated transport. Following is a brief introduction that should serve to get you confidently on your first bus, train, subway or L; all the systems are easy to use and become more so with familiarity. As is the case in many American cities, public transportation is not funded as well as it might be, but it does offer a reasonable and often very attractive alternative to traveling by private car.

Riding the CTA

With a few exceptions noted below, riding a bus or rail vehicle within the city costs the same whether you're going a block or 10 miles: you pay a standard fare ($1.50 as of 1999) that entitles you to ride until you reach your destination. If your destination requires that you transfer between conveyances, that costs an additional 30 cents. Transferring to a third conveyance is free, so long as your journey is completed within two hours of the time you began. This means that you can in fact make a round trip on a single fare plus transfer.

The preferred method of paying CTA fares is with a **Transit Card**, a magnetically encoded card that is available from vending machines at all subway and L stations, and (in certain fixed denominations) also at Jewel and Dominick's supermarkets. Cards can be encoded with value in any amount from $1.50 up to $100. Each time you begin a journey, the bus till or station turnstile that you use deducts the appropriate fare from your card. When you

Passengers wait for an elevated train in the Loop.

board a second transit vehicle within two hours of the beginning of a journey, the second vehicle deducts a transfer fare (30 cents) only. At any time you can "recharge" your card by inserting it into a Transit Card vending machine and adding more money. When you buy a new card or recharge a card, you get one free fare for each $13.50 on your card. This is in effect a volume discount.

You can also pay fares on a bus, L, or subway with a **token,** a special coin minted and sold by the CTA at its stations, at Currency Exchanges, and at some Jewel and Dominick's supermarkets. There is no volume discount for tokens, and it would not be surprising to see them eventually phased out completely and supplanted by Transit Cards. Finally, you can use cash to pay a regular or transfer fare on a bus, but you must have the correct change. Drivers don't handle money; the fares are deposited in an electronic till at the front of the bus, which also issues and accepts transfers. If you ride the CTA every day, to work or to school, you can get a monthly pass that is better value than a discount Transit Card. These are sold where tokens are sold.

Travel Strategy

Because of Chicago's grid layout, public transport tends to run in straight lines toward one of the cardinal points of the compass. With a few exceptions, every thoroughfare (the major street at every half-mile interval) has a bus route that travels back and forth on that street. So unless your destination lies on the same street where your journey begins, you will have to transfer to get where you want to go. The general exception to this rule is if your destination is the Loop, because all rapit transit trains (the collective name for Ls and subways) either terminate or pass through there, and many bus routes converge there.

The rapid transit system can be thought of as a hand with the palm situated in the Loop and the various lines radiating out from it like fingers. All lines either pass through the Loop or terminate there. The lines are identified by color, but the color naming scheme was only recently adopted, so you may hear people using the old names for various subway and L lines, which were mostly the names of the outermost stops: the Brown Line was the Ravenswood, the Yellow Line was the Skokie Swift, the Red Line was the Howard, and so forth.

If your journey requires a transfer, it will involve a wait somewhere. This will be a wait in absolutely frigid conditions for many months of the year, so if you don't like standing around in the cold, try to arrange your regular journeys in a way that enables you to complete the trip in a single bus or rapid transit ride.

All CTA trains and buses operate on a schedule; they are in principle supposed to be at a certain station or stop at a certain time. Owing to traffic and any number of other glitches that arise, vehicles may get out of synch with their schedules and start running late, to the point that a following vehicle catches up to the one in front. When this happens, drivers occasionally attempt to reestablish their correct position by running a bus or train "express"; that is, by skipping a number of stops until they catch up to the place where they should be. This maneuver defies the logic of what public transportation is supposed to do and by logical extension would lead to the possibility that all trains and buses could adhere perfectly to their schedules if they didn't stop to pick up passengers. Fortunately, this extreme has not been carried out! But you should not be surprised by an impromptu announcement that a bus or train is going to run "express" to a certain point. Be prepared to disembark if you learn that the station or stop where you would otherwise have gotten off is going to be skipped.

The best way to learn how to get around on the CTA is to use it. A free map is updated twice yearly by the CTA and is available at all rapid transit stations. The CTA's information line is (888) YOUR-CTA [(888) 967-7282].

Metra and Pace
Metra, when it was formed, incorporated half a dozen independent train companies operating a dozen commuter railways in the Chicagoland area. The new system of having a single authority and uniform fare structure is easy to use. All trains terminate downtown, at one of four rail stations:
- Northwestern Station on Canal between Madison and Lake Street, serving the north and northwest suburbs and southern Wisconsin
- Union Station, in the block bounded by Canal, Adams, Clinton, and Jackson Streets, serving northwest, southwest, and western suburbs
- La Salle Street Station, strangely located on Congress Parkway, serving the southwest suburbs
- Randolph Street Station, at Randolph Street and Michigan Avenue (trains can also be boarded at Van Buren and Michigan Avenue), serving the southern suburbs and northwest Indiana

Service on all suburban commuter lines is good at rush hours, spotty at other times, and often nonexistent on weekends. The system is designed mainly for those who work in downtown Chicago Monday to Friday during business hours and live outside the city. Information about schedules and fares on Metra and Pace is available at (312) 836-7000, a general information line that also gives CTA information.

Taxicabs

Being a taxi driver in Chicago is a time-honored entry-level job for uneducated immigrants; obtaining a cab license is not difficult, and there is nearly always a need for drivers. This means that your taxi driver may speak only the most rudimentary English, and he won't necessarily know the best way to get you to your destination—if indeed he even understands what you're saying! So if you know your way around, don't hesitate to tell a driver how to get to where you want to go. Taxi fares are all meter-based. There are premiums for extra baggage, extra passengers, and late-night journeys; the amounts for all of these show up on the meter. Every taxi is identified by number and the taxi driver is required to have his license prominently displayed on a frame in front of the glove compartment in the front seat. It is customary to tip taxi drivers 10–15 percent above the fare for good service, but you certainly shouldn't feel obliged to tip a driver who is discourteous or unhelpful.

All taxicabs are marked by bubble signs on the roof that are illuminated when the cab is available. A cab driver is obliged to stop and pick up any passenger who hails the cab, but drivers often pass up or ignore a fare that they suspect will take them to a part of the city that they don't wish to visit. All taxis are painted in uniform designs that identify the company they belong to; Yellow and Checker are the leaders, but there are many others. Cabs are generally plentiful downtown, in the Near North, and in North Side lakefront neighborhoods; they can be scarce elsewhere.

Where they are plentiful you can usually find one on the street; outside of these areas, it is a good idea to order one by phone. *Never* let your mobility depend completely on taxicabs if you live in a neighborhood where they are not plentiful. You can spend a very long time waiting and making follow-up calls for a cab that never comes if you live well off the beaten track.

DRIVING IN CHICAGO

In most respects Chicago is as car-friendly as other American cities, with the added bonus that it is relatively easy to navigate. The downsides of driving in Chicago are traffic congestion and the condition of the roads. For traffic congestion there is no remedy; if you drive, you will experience it from time to time, though certainly not to the degree common in more densely populated East Coast cities. All those bumps and jolts you encounter are the result of the freezing and thawing cycles during the winter months that leave a patchwork of cracks, seams, and potholes on the pavement. Maintaining the roads in any better condition would be unacceptably expensive for taxpayers and inconvenient for motorists; the only remedy is to get a car with a good suspension system. But first you need an Illinois driver's license.

Cars, Driving, and the Law

You cannot drive on your foreign driver's license legally as a resident of Illinois, so the best advice is to get an Illinois license as soon as possible. For any interim period you should obtain an international driving license in your own country before coming to the United States.

All legal matters relating to vehicles in Illinois are handled by the office of the Secretary of State, an elected government official. The State Government section of the telephone directory (blue pages) lists a general information number (nearly always busy) and the addresses of all city and suburban service centers that handle driver's licenses and related matters. You can get an application for a license by visiting any of these centers. To get a driver's license you will need to provide proof of your **legal name, date of birth, social security number, Illinois street address,** and **signature.** The conventional documents for proving these are mostly issued within the United States, so if you are backing your claim with foreign documents, such as a foreign driver's license and a foreign passport, be sure to take lots of supporting information with you.

Upon presentation of the proper documentation and application fee, you will be given a vision test and a written test, which can be taken in English, Spanish, or Korean; however, it is required that you understand all important road signs in English. If you pass these two tests you will be issued an **instruction permit,** also called a learner's permit, enabling you to drive legally as long as a responsible licensed driver is in the front passenger seat with you.

In order to get your full driver's license, you have to pass a **road test**, in a properly licensed and insured vehicle that you provide. This test is not as difficult or strict as it is in many countries. If you are a competent and experienced driver you will probably pass it the first time. However, you should acquaint yourself thoroughly with the driving laws of Illinois by picking up the free booklet *Rules of the Road,* which is available from offices of the Secretary of State. This booklet also contains detailed information about registering a vehicle and about insurance, which you will need to know if you buy a vehicle in the United States or if you import one from abroad.

A driver's license is the accepted form of identification all over the United States. If you don't drive and don't wish to learn, you can get a state-issued identification card from the same place you get a driver's license. The application process is similar (except that no testing is required) and you will need similar documentation.

Driving Laws That Affect You

There is no substitute for studying *Rules of the Road* in order to acquaint yourself thoroughly with laws that apply to drivers in Illinois. A few laws require special mention because they are very strictly enforced or because they are unique to the United States, Illinois, or Chicago. These include:

- **drinking and driving:** If your blood-alcohol concentration (BAC) is greater than 0.08 percent, or if any alcohol is found in your blood and you are judged to be driving with impaired ability, it is illegal for you to drive. DUI (driving under the influence) laws are very strictly enforced in Illinois and elsewhere in the United States; breaching them carries heavy fines and penalties, which may include the loss of your driving privileges.

- **driving on boulevards:** In the city of Chicago only, certain streets are designated as boulevards, either by having "boulevard" in the name of the street or by other signposting. It is illegal to drive a truck (including a pickup) or a commercial vehicle on a boulevard; such vehicles must use alternative routes.

- **mandatory insurance:** You cannot legally register or drive an uninsured vehicle in Illinois.

- **snow routes:** In Chicago and some other municipalities, you must remove your vehicle from a street designated as a snow route (the signs are obvious) when there are two inches or more of snow on the ground, even if your car is parked legally. This is in order to make way for snow removal equipment.

- **stopping for school buses:** A school bus has the authority to stop traffic behind and in front of it. Nearly all school buses are bright yellow with black trim. When a school bus is flashing red and amber lights, which it will do at least 100 feet in advance of stopping, you must stop your vehicle while students board or leave the bus. You can continue on your way when the flashing lights stop.

- **towing other vehicles:** A towed vehicle must be connected to a towing vehicle by a bar, reinforced by two chains or cables. Towing with a rope or other nonrigid device is illegal.
- **vehicle requirements:** Illinois vehicles are not subject to inspection as they are in many states, but they must be equipped with certain mandatory devices: study them in *Rules of the Road*. Periodically your vehicle must pass an emissions inspection to ensure it is not polluting unduly. You will be notified by mail about the details of this on any registered vehicle that you own.
- **yielding to pedestrians:** Pedestrians have the right-of-way over road vehicles in all reasonable circumstances. Pedestrians with plainly visible disabilities—those in wheelchairs, for example, or the blind—always have the right-of-way over vehicular traffic. Acquaint yourself with the details under "Pedestrian Right-of-Way" in *Rules of the Road*.

Car and Driving Tips

Gasoline (petrol) is cheap in the United States compared to many countries, and the price of it varies considerably from state to state, even from city to city, because different authorities have powers to tax it. Gasoline prices in Illinois are about average for the United States, but gas is expensive in Chicago; it gets more expensive as you get nearer the center of the city. If you have occasion to drive in the suburbs or even farther afield, buy your gas there rather than in the city; you can save as much as 25 cents a gallon. Gasoline is sold in gallons; a gallon is equal to 3.8 liters. Only unleaded gasoline in various grades is available; a number of vendors also sell diesel fuel. Most service stations are self-service, where you pump the gas yourself. You can pay with a credit card at the pump in most places. Stations identify self-service pumps with the word "self" and full-service pumps (where an attendant does all the work for you) with the word "full." You pay a hefty premium for full service, so don't pull up to a pump so marked if that isn't what you want.

You should always strictly obey parking regulations, and pay your tickets if you get any. Parking violation records are computerized. If you have a number outstanding, police will very likely find a convenient opportunity to immobilize or tow away your car.

In contrast to the system used in some countries, there is no delay in Chicago between the moment when traffic lights facing one way turn red and those facing the other way turn green; these events are usually simultaneous. Despite this, an alarming number of drivers try to extend the green by driving through the intersection as the light turns red. Always look out for these careless drivers, whether you're driving or walking; they are the cause of many accidents.

As a foreigner with no driving record in the United States and a new U.S. driver's license, you will have to pay relatively high insurance premiums to begin with; this is because insurance companies assume the worst about your driving in the absence of any hard facts. After you have driven for a year or so, it will pay you to shop around again for insurance coverage. If you have a good driving record, you will probably be able to find the same coverage for less money.

Cycling

Winter winds and snow are a definite drawback, but these aside, Chicago offers some of the best bicycling of any large American city. A continuous, 18.5-mile bicycle trail along the lakefront is unsurpassed for views of both the lake and the people there to enjoy it. Cycling is also permitted on all Chicago streets except expressways, but

most of these do not have set-aside bicycle lanes. Cyclists must practice constant vigilance to avoid careless motorists. Riding without a helmet is foolish; if you ride frequently the odds favor your taking a spill at some point, either because of road conditions or a driver who didn't see you.

Cyclists are required to obey all the traffic signals, safety laws, and rules that apply to vehicle drivers. If you will ever cycle after dark, make sure your bicycle is equipped with reflectors and lights. A bell or horn is also an essential accessory, since many bicycle paths are shared with slower pedestrians and in-line skaters.

Walkabout

There are sidewalks everywhere in Chicago and beautiful pathways all along the lakefront that make for pleasant walking. A few of the newer suburbs, where the car is king, make no provision for pedestrians at all, assuming that everyone will travel by car. Because Chicago is so big and spread out, it's not a place where you can expect to be able to walk to work or school, unless you purposefully choose a place to live that permits this; and in any case, walking outdoors during the winter months is not very pleasant, and can even be hazardous where sidewalks are not cleared of ice and snow.

You should avoid *jaywalking*, that is crossing the street at a place other than an intersection or a marked pedestrian crosswalk. Jaywalking is officially against the law, but it is quite common — just not very safe. Hitchhiking has fallen from fashion in the United States and certainly within cities. You're not likely to attract the attention of anyone but the police if you try to flag down a ride within the metropolitan area.

CHAPTER FOUR

A PLACE TO CALL HOME

When I visit any other great city of the world, I am a guest.
When I am in Chicago, I am at home.

— Sherwood Anderson

WHERE TO LIVE?

Whether you are going to buy or rent a place to live, you probably want to decide first where you want to call home; this will simplify your housing search considerably. You can start by drawing up a list of concerns that you can rank according to their importance to you. Here are some of the things you'll want to consider, along with some background that will help you decide what is most important:

Education: if you have school-age children, chances are that your main concern will be to live in a good school district. In general terms, all suburban schools are better than City of Chicago public schools, except for the city's special schools: the magnet schools and the high schools catering to gifted students, or those concentrating their education early in a particular field (these are discussed in more detail in Chapter 9). As you would expect, the best public schools are located in the wealthiest suburbs that have the highest property taxes.

Local Color: Chicago is a city of neighborhoods, each with its own character. While many Chicago neighborhoods are quite diverse, there is usually an underlying pattern of birds of a feather flocking together. The unifying elements can be age, ethnic background, income, sexual orientation, or marital status. If you have strong feelings about the sort of people you want for neighbors, this concern will go at the top of your list.

Noise: If you fancy coming home to peace and quiet every evening, avoid Chicago's main noisemakers: the major thoroughfares, which are conduits for traffic day and night and are almost never quiet, and the elevated trains, which cause a racket that sounds like the end of the world if you have one running by your apartment. If you're near a major hospital or a fire station, sirens will be a regular feature, and some neighborhoods near the two main airports suffer considerably from the rumble of constant air traffic.

Parking: If you're going to rely mainly on a car to get around, think about where you'll park it. On-street parking is available nearly everywhere in Chicago, but hard to find downtown, in the Near North, in Hyde Park, and along the lakefront. Some neighborhoods have permit parking, which reserves the most desirable parking places for people who live in the neighborhood. This is good for you but bad for anyone who may want to visit you and is unable to find a space. Apartment buildings with their own parking lots are more expensive and in some cases you will have to pay for parking in addition to your rent, but most people would agree it is well worth the money. You will probably have to locate in the suburbs or well away from the lake and downtown if you want your own private garage. Alternatively, you can rent a space by the month or longer period in a public garage. If you drive an expensive, late-model, or newer foreign car, it will be worth your while to pay for off-street parking, to protect it from the ravages of weather, vandalism, and theft.

Security: Crimes against people and property are highest in Chicago's poor, all-black neighborhoods on the South and West Sides, but muggings and burglaries can and do happen anywhere in the city. The burglary rate for apartments drives many people (who can afford it) into buildings with doormen, which are generally safe from such predations. If your dwelling will be empty for large parts of the day, give a thought to how tempting it may be to criminals and what resources are available to you to protect it.

Shopping and Amenities: Before you settle on a place to live, survey the local shopping to make sure you'll find everything you need. Supermarkets are located in all parts of the city, but the merchandise they carry gets a local flavor influenced by ethnicity and economics. You may also want to consider proximity to services such as daycare, a library, and recreational facilities.

Transportation: If you are going to use public transportation, think about what your main journeys will be and try to locate yourself where you need to take only *one* ride to get to where you want to go—one bus or one train. If you need to transfer, the trip will be considerably slower. If public transportation is going to be your only transportation, think about locating where you have a choice of ways to reach your regular destinations; if your mobility depends on one particular bus or train, you could find yourself occasionally stranded.

COMMUNITY LOCATOR

Advertising for properties, both for rent or for sale, appears widely: in the daily press, in the Chicago *Reader* (a free weekly; see Chapter 10); in the Sunday papers, where there is a real estate section of special interest to homebuyers; and in hundreds of sites on the World Wide Web. Use a search engine to zero in on "real estate" and "Chicago" or "Chicagoland."

Real estate listings are generally by neighborhood name within the city, and by suburb name outside the city limits. The sheer number of names and the failure of advertisers to note whether an address is inside or outside the city of Chicago (they expect you to know that!) can be a bit frustrating for the newcomer. Following are two tables that list (1) the common names for Chicago neighborhoods and communities, with location information within the city, and (2) the names of Chicago suburbs, with location information in relation to Chicago. Remarks, where pertinent for the house-hunter, are included.

Chicago Neighborhoods

"Near" in the following table means in relation to the Chicago Loop, downtown. There is lately a tendency for new neighborhood names to be invented by realtors (the official name for real estate agents), developers, and other marketing types who are promoting new housing developments in reclaimed industrial, derelict, or neglected neighborhoods. These "communities," some of which don't have any real community life as yet, tend to offer modern, pleasant, and generally fairly pricey housing. They are marked by an asterisk.

The table does not include all Chicago neighborhoods, only those used in advertisements for housing. Neighborhoods that are not given any "remarks" can be assumed to be typical: middle income, mostly ordinary Americans with an ethnic mix representative of the population as a whole.

79

The few neighborhoods with "Harbor" in the name (Diversey Harbor, Belmont Harbor, Burnham Harbor) are near those respective harbors on the lakefront. Generally tall apartment buildings, and generally pricey.

Neighborhood	Location	Remarks
Albany Park	northwest	noticeable Korean presence
Andersonville	north	formerly Swedish, now ethnic smorgasbord
Archer Heights	southwest	residents of Polish descent; there aren't actually any "heights."
Austin	west	all black
Avalon Park	southeast	all black
Avondale	northwest	
Belmont Cragin	northwest	nearly all white
Beverly	south	
Bridgeport	near southwest	near Comiskey Park, home of the Chicago White Sox
Bucktown	northwest	adjacent to Wicker Park and very much like it
Buena Park	north	some lake frontage
Burnham Park*	near south	mostly newly created housing
Burnside	southeast	mostly black
Calumet Heights	southeast	mostly black
Chatham	south	all black
Chicago Lawn	southwest	low- to middle-income
Chinatown	near south	like the name sounds
Clearing	southwest	all white; contains part of Midway Airport and lots of railroad tracks

Neighborhood	Location	Remarks
DePaul	northwest	around DePaul University, centered around Fullerton and Sheffield
Douglas	south	large black majority; includes Prairie Shores and Lake Meadows, which were attempts at integrated housing
Downtown	central	the Loop and immediate surrounding area
Dunning	northwest	Poles and Italians in good supply
East Side	south	working-class ethnic mix; borders Indiana
Edgewater	north	the lakefront from Irving Park to Devon; expensive on the water, funkier a bit inland with more ethnic variety
Edison Park	northwest	all white
Forest Glen	northwest	all white
Fuller Park	south	all black
Garfield Park	west	all black
Garfield Ridge	southwest	contains part of Midway Airport
Gold Coast	near north	the lakefront from Oak Street to North Avenue and a bit inland; the most expensive and exclusive area of Chicago
Grand Crossing	south	all black
Hegewisch	southeast	mostly white, low- to middle-income
Hermosa	northwest	strong Puerto Rican presence
Humboldt Park	northwest	largely Latino
Hyde Park	southeast	home of the University of Chicago; the only major Southside neighborhood not predominantly black
Irving Park	northwest	mostly white
Jefferson Park	northwest	mostly white

Neighborhood	Location	Remarks
Kenwood	southeast	integrated with black majority; north of Hyde Park
Lakeview	north	the lakefront from Diversey to Irving Park Road; fashionable for young professionals and gays
Lawndale	west	divided between blacks (north) and Mexicans (south)
Lincoln Park	near north	Armitage to Diversey along the lake; lots of restaurants and nightlife, popular with professionals
Lincoln Square	north	sizable Latino minority
Little Italy	near southwest	more Italian businesses than Italian residents
Little Village	southwest	largely Mexican and other Latino
Logan Square	northwest	formerly Polish, becoming more Latino
Loop	central	most housing is expensive condos and apartments
Lower West Side	west	mainly Mexican
Loyola Park	north	near Loyola University, 6400 N on the lakefront
Marquette Park	southwest	near Midway; Chicago's Lithuanian stronghold
Montclare	northwest	mostly white
Morgan Park	south	
Near North Side	north	mostly pricey newer or converted housing
Near South Side	south	becoming more fashionable, with many loft conversions
Near West Side	west	all black on western side; expensive and fashionable nearer the Loop

Neighborhood	Location	Remarks
North Center	north	
North Park	northwest	Koreans on the rise
Norwood Park	northwest	all white
Oakland	south	all black
Old Town	near north	single professionals and young marrieds
Pilsen	near southwest	largely Mexican, including many immigrants
Portage Park	northwest	mostly white
Printers' Row*	near south	newer conversions and apartment complexes
Pullman	southeast	historic preservation district, ethnically mixed
Ravenswood	north	family neighborhood, mixture of houses and apartments
Riverdale	southeast	mostly black
River North*	near north	newly developed and fashionable
River West*	near northwest	reclaimed industrial, around Clybourn Avenue near the Chicago River; newly developed and fashionable
Rogers Park	north	Devon to city limit along the lake; Jews, Latinos, Russian immigrants, students
Roseland	south	mostly black
Sandburg Village	near north	a collection of apartments on Clark between North and Division
South Chicago	southeast	working-class ethnic mix; many industrial areas
South Deering	southeast	working-class ethnic mix, mostly black and Latino

Neighborhood	Location	Remarks
South Loop	near south	new and converted housing, some with river frontage
South Shore	southeast	middle-income black neighborhood on the lakefront
Streeterville	near north	east of North Michigan Avenue, and mostly fantastically expensive
Ukrainian Village	near west	The Ukrainians have mostly left and been replaced by an eclectic low- to middle-income mix.
Uptown	north	the North Side's least glamorous, most multicultural, and cheapest neighborhood
West Lawn	southwest	nearly all white
West Ridge	north	strong Jewish presence
Wicker Park	near northwest	recently gentrified, lots of artists, musicians, and wannabes
Woodlawn	southeast	mostly black
Wrigleyville	near northwest	around Wrigley Field, where the Chicago Cubs play

Chicago Suburbs

In this table "near" means near the city limits of Chicago, adjacent or separated by not more than one other suburb. "Far" means quite distant from Chicago, about as far as you can go and still be considered in the suburbs. "Near O'Hare" or "near Midway" can be translated as "many planes flying over." The suburbs are in general more prosperous and more white than neighborhoods in Chicago. Exceptions to the rule are noted. Suburbs with $ in the remarks column are the ten most wealthy. "Prosperous" means the average house costs at least $175,000. The list does not include *all* suburbs; there are more than two hundred. These are the larger and better known ones.

Chicago and its suburbs

85

Suburb	Location	Remarks
Addison	far west	
Alsip	south	
Arlington Heights	northwest	home of a well-known racetrack
Aurora	far west	a separate city that has become a suburb
Bannockburn	north	$
Barrington	northwest	prosperous
Barrington Hills	northwest	$
Bartlett	far west	
Batavia	far west	
Bedford Park	near southwest	near Midway
Bellwood	west	middle-income, integrated suburb
Bensenville	near northwest	near O'Hare
Berwyn	near west	Czech, Slovak, Polish, and Italian are the main flavors
Bloomingdale	west	
Blue Island	near south	
Bolingbrook	far southwest	
Bridgeview	near southwest	near Midway
Brookfield	west	home of Brookfield Zoo, largest in the Chicago area
Buffalo Grove	northwest	strong Eastern European descent
Burbank	near southwest	
Calumet City	near south	low- to middle-income, ethnically mixed

Suburb	Location	Remarks
Carol Stream	west	
Carpentersville	far west	
Chicago Heights	far south	middle-income, ethnically mixed
Chicago Ridge	near south	
Cicero	near west	increasing Mexican minority; Czechs and Slovaks as well
Country Club Hills	south	middle-income, ethnically mixed
Crestwood	south	
Crystal Lake	far northwest	
Darien	west	
Deerfield	north	prosperous
Des Plaines	northwest	near O'Hare
Dolton	near south	middle-income, ethnically mixed
Downers Grove	far west	
Elgin	far west	a separate city that has become a suburb
Elk Grove Village	northwest	near O'Hare
Elmhurst	west	
Elmwood Park	near west	strong Italian accent
Evanston	near north	first northern suburb on the lake, home of Northwestern University
Evergreen Park	near southwest	
Flossmoor	far south	
Forest Park	near west	middle-income, ethnically mixed
Franklin Park	near west	near O'Hare with growing ethnic influx

Suburb	Location	Remarks
Glencoe	north	$, on the lakefront
Glen Ellyn	west	
Glenview	north	prosperous
Glenwood	far south	growing ethnic influx
Hanover Park	far west	
Harvey	south	largely black
Hazel Crest	south	becoming largely black
Hickory Hills	west	
Highland Park	north	prosperous, on the lakefront
Hinsdale	west	
Hoffman Estates	northwest	
Homewood	south	
Joliet	far southwest	a separate city that has become a suburb
Kenilworth	north	$, on the lakefront
LaGrange	west	
LaGrange Park	west	
Lake Bluff	far north	on the lakefront
Lake Forest	far north	$, on the lakefront; home of Lake Forest College
Lansing	far south	middle-income
Libertyville	northwest	prosperous
Lincolnwood	near north	prosperous
Lisle	west	
Lombard	far west	
Long Grove	northwest	$

Suburb	Location	Remarks
Markham	south	mostly black
Maywood	near west	becoming mostly black
Melrose Park	west	
Mettawa	north	$
Midlothian	southwest	
Morton Grove	near north	
Mount Prospect	northwest	
Mundelein	northwest	
Naperville	far west	prosperous
Niles	near north	
Norridge	near northwest	near O'Hare
Northbrook	north	prosperous
North Chicago	far north	on the lakefront; middle-income, ethnically mixed
Northlake	near west	growing Latino minority
Oakbrook	west	$
Oak Forest	southwest	
Oak Lawn	near southwest	
Oak Park	near west	thought of as a model integrated community; many Frank Lloyd Wright houses
Orland Park	far southwest	
Palatine	northwest	
Palos Heights	southwest	
Palos Hills	southwest	

Suburb	Location	Remarks
Park Forest	south	
Park Ridge	near northwest	prosperous, near O'Hare
Prospect Heights	northwest	prosperous
Riverdale	near south	
River Forest	near west	prosperous, strong Irish presence
Rolling Meadows	northwest	
Roselle	northwest	
Rosemont	northwest	near O'Hare; home to a major sports and entertainment pavillion and a convention center
Schaumburg	northwest	
Schiller Park	near northwest	near O'Hare
Skokie	near north	large Jewish population
South Barrington	northwest	$
South Holland	south	
St. Charles	far west	a separate town that has become a suburb
Streamwood	far northwest	
Tinley Park	southwest	
Villa Park	west	
Waukegan	far north	on the lakefront
Westchester	west	
West Chicago	far west	
Western Springs	west	prosperous
Westmont	west	

Suburb	Location	Remarks
Wheaton	far west	a separate town that has become a suburb
Wheeling	northwest	
Wilmette	near north	prosperous, on the lakefront
Winnetka	north	$, on the lakefront
Woodridge	far west	
Woodstock	far northwest	a separate town that has become a suburb
Zion	far north	

TYPES OF HOUSING

The main distinction in housing type is between houses and apartments. A **house** has its own door to the street and is usually free-standing, though in a few areas of Chicago there are houses that share one or two walls with neighboring houses. These are usually called **townhouses** or **town homes** and are what you may think of as terraced houses. In Chicagoland they tend to be of newer construction, especially in the suburbs, though there are a few older ones in the city. An **apartment** is a dwelling within a building that has accommodation for more than one household. It is possible though not usual for an apartment to have its own door to the street. Apartments are offered for rent (paid monthly) throughout Chicagoland. A **condominium** (**condo** for short) is an apartment that is owned outright rather than rented from a landlord. Both condos and apartments are what much of the English-speaking world calls flats.

Condos and apartments are advertised mainly by size. A **studio** is a one-room apartment that will also have a bathroom (containing toilet, sink, and shower and/or bathtub) and a corner or alcove with cooking facilities. A **convertible** apartment is a studio with an alcove that may be used as a sleeping or dining area, though

91

it is not considered a separate room because it doesn't have a separate door. Larger apartments and condos are advertised by the number of bedrooms they contain, usually up to three. A one-bedroom apartment or condo can be expected to have a bedroom, a bathroom, a kitchen, a living room, and a dining room or at least a dining area near the kitchen. Apartments come in buildings of all sizes. A **two-flat** or a **three-flat** is a building that contains two or three apartments, respectively. A **loft** is an apartment in a converted, formerly industrial building. A **courtyard building** has several doors opening onto a courtyard that faces the street on one side, each door leading to multiple apartments. **High-rises** are tall apartment buildings. These are common near and on the lakefront. They have from two to several apartments per floor, accessed by elevators. The higher the floor, the more expensive the rent or selling price.

A North Side courtyard building.

Houses in Chicagoland come in all shapes and sizes. Starting at the small end, the most typical is the **bungalow**, a small, one-story, free-standing house (of which there are thousands on the southwest side). A **Victorian** is a house around 100 years old (or a newer house in this style) of brick or wood frame construction, two stories at least, and often with ornate, decorative wood features inside and out. A **Queen Anne** is less ornate than a Victorian, but similar in style and often includes a wrap-around porch. A **ranch house**, or **rancher**, is a one-story, relatively modern house in a rectangular or L-shape, more spacious than a bungalow and likely to have an attached garage. Ranchers (and the two following types as well) are almost nonexistent in Chicago but common in the suburbs. A **Cape Cod** is usually a 1.5-story, wood-frame construction with a gabled roof and dormer windows. A **colonial** is rectangular, usually two stories, with sash windows divided into small panes and typically with fireplaces.

Real estate advertising uses a lot of shorthand codes that, if not familiar, may cause you to think that accommodation is being advertised without revealing pertinent facts about it. Following is a table containing terms found frequently in housing ads, along with their longhand translations.

Term	Meaning
ac	air conditioning
appliances	cooking stove and refrigerator
assessments	the value assigned to a property for the calculation of property tax
back porch	in an apartment building, a roofed rear stairwell with a landing large enough for a table and chairs for outdoor dining
block	the distance from one street to the next
br	bedroom
ca	central air conditioning

Term	Meaning
cable	wiring is provided for cable TV; inquire who pays the subscription cost
cathedral ceiling	high vaulted ceiling
central air	central air conditioning
(central) heat	ambiguous, since no dwelling could reasonably be without it; inquire for particulars
conversion	a building built for something else, now divided into apartments or condos
deck	an outdoor wooden platform at floor level for sitting outside or dining in good weather
dishwasher	automatic dishwashing machine
eat-in kitchen	kitchen big enough for a dining table
Eurokitchen or Eurostyle kitchen	a marketing buzzword. Ask what it means. Typically it means all appliances are white, built-in, and very close together.
FSBO	for sale by owner — no agents involved
full amenities	usually means doorman, garage, and laundry facilities at least; inquire for specifics.
gut rehab	a building that has been completely rebuilt on the inside
half-bath	sink and toilet, no shower or bathtub
hardwoods	hardwood floors
hutch	built-in cabinet with glass front for dishes, knick-knacks, or whatever
hwfl	hardwood floors
landmark	a building that somebody thinks is architecturally interesting or significant
laundry	a washer and dryer in a house; a laundry room with coin-operated machines in an apartment building
parking	usually means private, off-street parking, but inquire
plus utilities	you pay for electricity, natural gas, and telephone in addition to the rent

Term	Meaning
rehabbed	a formerly rundown or derelict building that has been remodeled
storage	an area usually in the basement of an apartment building divided into storage closets
sublet	you rent from people who are themselves already tenants, not owners
vintage	old and appreciably ornate
wbfp	wood-burning fireplace
w/d	washer/dryer
yard	area in front, back, or side planted in lawn

RENTING A PROPERTY

Residential rentals come in all sizes and shapes throughout Chicagoland. In the city most rentals are apartments, but there are also houses available, especially in neighborhoods away from the lakefront. In the suburbs, especially newer and more distant ones, houses and townhouses are more common than large apartment buildings. Among large American cities Chicago enjoys one of the amplest and best maintained stocks of residential housing, which has the happy effect of making accommodation cheaper, more spacious, and of better quality than you are likely to find in America's East Coast cities.

The vast majority of rentals are unfurnished, meaning that the house or apartment is empty but for fixtures, and usually a stove and refrigerator. There are, however, some mostly luxury apartments that are rented fully furnished for short-stay executives and jet-setters.

You can engage the services of an agent to find an apartment or house to rent if you don't have much time to look around yourself and if you would like somebody else to do the initial research, but this isn't really necessary. The rental market is big and user-friendly. By educating yourself about it a little up front, you can probably find out most of the things you need to know. The best way to learn about a particular property is by talking with the landlord on the telephone first: then you can use your time to see only the properties that interest you. You will probably save a lot of time in your search by settling on the area you want to live in first, but it will also pay you to make a list of exactly what it is you want in a house or apartment. That way you can eliminate a majority of advertised properties from consideration.

As a foreigner in Chicago with no established credit history (see chapter 7) you may have to provide more in the way of security and documentation than an American would for renting the same property. At the very least you should have documentation showing your residency status in the United States and a letter that confirms your work or student status. You may have to pay as much as double the usual amount of security deposit.

Rents vary widely depending on location, age and quality of the building or house, and size of the accommodation. A two-bedroom house in an outlying neighborhood that is not very close to a train or L may cost as little as $800 a month, while a studio in

a Near North luxury high-rise may run as high as $1,500 a month. Suburban accommodation is in general cheaper than comparable city accommodation, but if you work or study in Chicago you will have to consider the cost of commuting, as well as the time it takes. Generally, there is accommodation to suit every budget and taste. Whether your taste will conform to the restrictions of your budget is something you'll have to discover.

In the city of Chicago, all rental properties (except those in owner-occupied buildings with less than six units) are governed by a city ordinance that defines the landlord-tenant relationship. You can acquaint yourself with the details of the law if you wish by getting a copy at the office of the City Clerk in City Hall. It is a good idea to know what your rights are, especially if you end up with a landlord who doesn't want to hold up his end of the bargain as regards repairs or heating, for example.

Most landlords all over Chicagoland, whether individuals or companies, use a standard lease that is a legally binding contract. You will have to sign it. *Read it first!* You do not have to sign it on the spot when you agree to rent a property. If you do not know how long you want to stay in a property, it is better to get a lease shorter than the time you expect rather than longer. If there is any possibility that you will have to leave the property before the end of the lease, you will still be responsible for the rent to the end of the lease, or alternatively, you will be responsible for subletting the apartment, which may involve costs. You should acquaint yourself with all the language in the lease and ask questions about any parts of it that are unclear or that seem draconian. While the cost of rent is usually not negotiable, some clauses in a lease may be. It is possible that you can get your landlord to eliminate or alter conditions that you are not comfortable with. Leases normally run for one year. During the period of a lease your rent should not increase, but make sure that this fact is spelled out in the lease. You can be almost certain that if you have an option to

A three-flat with windows in characteristic Chicago architectural style.

renew a lease, your rent will go up by at least the amount of infla-
tion on renewal. Leases typically begin on May 1 and October 1,
making these two dates very busy around the city for people moving in and out. Avoid them if you can by getting a lease with a
different starting date.

BUYING A PROPERTY

You may decide it is to your advantage to buy a property in
Chicagoland. The chief advantages are that you are acquiring an
investment that is very likely to appreciate, and that you will gain
considerable tax advantages. Interest you pay on your mortgage
and your property taxes are largely tax-deductible. The disadvantages are reduced freedom and mobility, and the likelihood of
greater expenses. In addition to your mortgage payment you have
the cost of all utilities, of maintenance on your property, and if
you buy a condominium, of management fees for the building or
complex you live in. Whether you buy a house or a condo, you
will have to pay property taxes. These are not a trivial matter.
Taxes on a three- or four-bedroom house in one of the wealthier
suburbs can be $10,000 a year or more. Be sure to take into ac-
count the property taxes of any property you view when deciding
whether you can afford it.

An unlimited array of professionals is already lined up to
assist you in the enterprise of buying a residence and we cannot
hope to compete with their expertise, so here is a brief primer on
the process. Residential properties for sale—whether houses or
condos—are advertised through real estate agents, in newspapers,
and through free publications that consist entirely of property ads
(available at real estate agents and from boxes on busy street
corners). People selling privately, without the use of agencies,
advertise in small ads in newpapers and on the Internet. You may
want to peruse all of these to find your dream house, but the best
way to start is to engage an agent. If you want to begin your search

before you arrive in Chicago, check out any of the numerous real estate listings on the World Wide Web; most large U.S. agencies have all of their listings available, along with pictures and other information. Use a search engine to find real estate in Illinois, and narrow your search to a community or area.

Properties for sale are normally listed only with a single agent, but all agents have access to all listings via a computerized system called the MLS (Multiple Listing System). Traditionally a single agent who listed a property acted as a go-between in transactions between the homebuyer and seller. Increasingly now both the buyer and the seller are represented by agents, and these agents split the commission payable when a house is sold. The commission is calculated as a percentage of the selling cost and thus always comes out of the seller's pocket. It is to your advantage to find an agent to represent you as a homebuyer; it costs you nothing and provides you with a professional who is devoting time to getting you what you want out of the deal—a new home. The buyer already has such a professional working for him or her: the listing agent. If you deal only with a listing agent you are in effect consorting with the enemy, for this agent wants to realize the highest price possible for the property and is not obligated to tell you everything he or she may know about it or about the sellers.

An agent that you engage to represent you—usually called a **Buyer's Agent**—can show you any property that is listed with MLS, provided that your agent's agency subscribes to the MLS, and you should make sure that it does. You can give your agent a profile of the kind of property you are looking for, or you can find properties yourself through the outlets mentioned above and then have your agent arrange a showing for you. If you have engaged a buyer's agent, you should not deal with the listing agent of any property directly; your agent will do that.

A contract to buy a house originates with the buyer. Forms are standard throughout Chicago. In the suburbs, individual communities may have different standard contracts, depending on municipal or county laws. All details of the contract will be looked after by your agent. You are welcome to engage an independent attorney to look over a housing contract for you if you are in any doubt as to the meaning or intent of any clause; remember that your agent is not a lawyer. In the time between when you make an initial offer and when your offer is accepted by the buyer, your agent and the listing agent will work out all of the details concerning price, repairs to be carried out, and other conditions that may apply. You do not deal with the seller directly, and you may not even deal directly with the listing agent. For this reason, it is important to make sure that your agent knows *exactly* what you want so that he or she represents you properly. Your only direct encounter with the seller may be at the **closing** (also called **settlement**), when money, ownership, and keys change hands.

Financing

At the same time you look for a property to buy you should talk to a lender: a bank, savings and loan association, or mortgage broker. If you are a foreigner without a long-established record of credit in the United States, this is especially important because it may take a lender longer to determine that you are creditworthy. Traditionally people approach their own bank or savings institution to obtain a mortgage, but increasingly today, companies specializing in selling mortgages offer very competitive deals. These companies advertise in newspapers, on the Web, on billboards, and in the Yellow Pages under "mortgage."

When you settle on a lender, they will provide you with a very valuable and free booklet published by the U.S. Department of Housing and Urban Development (HUD) called *Buying Your Home: Settlement Costs and Helpful Information*. This book is so helpful that you should try to get your hands on one before you even settle on a lender. (One way to do this is to visit HUD's website, **www.hud.gov**, where you will find screen and downloadable versions of this and many other publications relating to housing.) The booklet goes into considerable detail about the legal aspects of buying residential property that are standard throughout the United States and also indicates the aspects of it that are likely to vary from state to state. In broad terms, the buying and selling of homes is governed by legislation called RESPA, the Real Estate Settlement Procedures Act, which came into being mainly to put an end to unscrupulous practices in property selling. The legislation is in place to protect sellers and especially buyers. It is to your advantage to acquaint yourself with its main features.

Getting Insurance

If you have bought a property your lender will have given you information about proper insurance for your house; it is required to be in place before the closing of the deal. If you are renting a property you can still insure your own possessions against loss, theft, damage, and the like, though you are not required to do so. See the "Insurance Agents" listing in the Yellow Pages or consult your neighbors about a reputable company.

Connecting to Services

Unless you are moving into a new suburban home, the place you move into will probably already have all required services connected; that is, electricity, natural gas, telephone, and water. Your only job is to ensure that all accounts are transferred to your name, and that there are no outstanding bills for services to your address from previous owners or tenants.

Electricity: All of northeastern Illinois is supplied by Commonwealth Edison (Com Ed for short), a regulated monopoly company. You can call their free telephone number, (800) 334-7661, to arrange for electrical service. Electricity is standard throughout the United States: 110–120 volts, 60 Hz, alternating current (AC).

Gas: Another regulated monopoly company, People's Gas, supplies natural gas to all of Chicagoland. Their telephone number is (312) 240-7000; or see the numbers in the telephone directory (white pages) under People's Gas.

Telephone: Local telephone service, as of 1999, is provided to Chicagoland by Ameritech, one of the "Baby Bells" (companies formed after the breakup of the former monopoly AT&T). You can order new or changed service on their free number, (800) 244-4444. The telecommunications industry is in upheaval, and before long, other companies may be able to compete in the now controlled local telephone market. You should ask your neighbors or read the press for the latest information about local service.

When you establish local service, you must also indicate to Ameritech which long-distance carrier you wish to use. There is a wide variety of choice. All of the major long-distance companies offer incentives to attract new business, and all of them are constantly reorganizing their service to make it cheaper—or at least to make it seem cheaper. If you are going to be making frequent calls abroad or to other parts of the United States, it will pay you to get specifics from all the major long-distance companies before choosing one. The most popular long-distance carriers are MCI, Sprint, and AT&T, but many smaller companies offer competitive service at cheaper rates. Consult the daily press to learn how to contact these companies; they all advertise heavily.

Other decisions to be made about your telephone service concern which extra services you want. The telephone company will want to sell you all of them, so it may be useful for you to consider in advance which might be suitable. The most common services are:

- *call waiting:* lets you know, when you are speaking on the telephone, that another caller is trying to reach you.
- *call forwarding:* enables you to "send" your incoming calls to another number when you are not at home.

103

- *caller ID:* identifies the source of incoming calls on a small device. It doesn't always work for long-distance calls, and doesn't work for international calls.
- *call block:* prevents calls being made to your phone from certain telephone numbers that you supply.
- *voice mail:* takes the place of a telephone answering machine.

This is only a small selection; see the front of the telephone directory (white pages) for many more options.

U.S. phone numbers consist of ten digits, of which the first three are the **area code**. Chicagoland has five area codes: 312 for central Chicago, 773 immediately surrounding the center, and 847, 630, and 708 for the surrounding suburbs. Farther afield than this is area 815, covering the rest of northern Illinois. You can reach another number within your area code by dialing the last seven digits only. To call a number outside your area code, dial 1 plus the ten-digit number that includes the other area code. Telephone numbers beginning with 800 and 888 are toll-free calls, that is, long-distance calls that are treated as local calls for billing purposes.

Most people buy their own telephones; it's cheaper than renting the telephone company's equipment. Telephones are widely available in electronics and appliance stores. A substantial number of people also do their own telephone wiring; all of the supplies are readily available, along with instruction books.

Mobile telephones are available from a great number of companies that are in fierce competition and advertise widely.

Water: The City of Chicago supplies water within the city limits to all businesses and residences. It is not metered and is not paid for separately, but rather through taxation. Water in all the other suburbs is a local affair, so if you settle outside of Chicago you should consult your neighbors to learn what authority supplies water and how you pay for it.

Garbage Collection: The City of Chicago handles waste collection in the city and pays for it through taxation. As with water, garbage collection in the suburbs is a local affair; consult neighbors to learn who takes it away and who pays for it. Whether you are in city or suburbs, collection is usually once a week. Neighbors are the best source of information about that, as well as about recycling programs, which are normally administered by the same entities that collect garbage.

Internet: A large number of Internet access companies operate in Chicagoland: some local, some regional, some national. These days basic service usually means an email address, server space for your own web page, and some access agreement: either unlimited, or for a fixed number of hours per month, above which you pay a premium. You should ensure that your Internet service provider will be a local, not a long-distance call for you. If you are going to be traveling frequently, either in the United States or abroad, it is probably worthwhile to get an account with one of the national companies, CompuServe or America Online. They have local dial-up numbers in nearly every part of the world, making it easy and cheap for you to send and receive email from anywhere.

Getting Domestic Help

A majority of Americans do not employ domestic help—even when they could afford to so. Nearly everything Americans eat and use at home is designed to require minimum preparation, care, and maintenance. Thus even a busy family, where both adults work, can find time to keep up their house *and* find leisure time to enjoy themselves. Having domestic help is not unheard of though and it is becoming more common, especially among city and suburban professional families where both parents have careers. There are a number of agencies that provide cleaning services, and if you don't get a personal recommendation from somebody, these agencies are a reliable place to find a worker to clean your house. Most of the people who work in this trade in Chicagoland are Polish and Latino women. You can contact agencies that supply them by looking under "House Cleaning" or "Maid & Butler Service" in the Yellow Pages.

Your Address and Mail

All of the parts of your address will probably be known to you by the time you move in, except perhaps your ZIP code—the five- or nine-digit number that the post office uses to sort mail. You can learn your ZIP code from neighbors or, if you live within the city limits, from the street guide in the front of the Chicago Yellow Pages. After you have moved in and received at least one piece of mail, you may get a form from your local letter carrier asking you to identify yourself and all of the people at your address who will be receiving mail there. This form is not used by anyone other than the post office.

It is useful to keep bills that show your name and address on them; they may be required to prove that you live where you say you do, for example when you apply to a store for credit.

Mail is delivered once a day, six times a week (not on Sundays) all over the United States. It may not come until very late in the day. If you are not home to receive a parcel or registered letter, you will be left a form giving you the option of picking it up at a post office (probably not very near by) or requesting redelivery. There is nearly always a long wait at post offices to do anything, so the fewer trips you can make there, the less your patience will be taxed.

If you need an address where you can receive mail before you actually arrive in Chicago and do not have contacts who can receive mail for you, you can use a private service that receives and holds mail for individuals or businesses. Look in the Yellow Pages under "Mail Boxes."

CHAPTER FIVE

HEALTH
AND SAFETY

*You can get much further with a smile, a kind word, and a
gun than you can get with a smile and a kind word.*
— Al Capone, legendary Chicago gangster

Hollywood has created a lurid image of American life that everyone agrees is quite exciting on the silver screen but less appealing
at street level. The popular image is largely untrue, and first-time
visitors to the United States are often pleasantly surprised to find
that people do not all have pistols next to their pillows, or walk
the streets in fear. The popular perception of healthcare in America,
on the other hand, is probably closer to reality. It is a high-tech,
high-quality, state-of-the-art industry that serves those who pay
for it very well but sadly neglects some others who can't afford to
use it.

This chapter will guide you through the labyrinth of the healthcare system and provide advice on how to be safe and secure in your castle, or on the street in Chicago.

PERSONAL AND FAMILY HEALTHCARE

Next to finding and settling into your new home, sorting out your healthcare may well be the most formidable task of your transition to life in Chicago. Mind you, it doesn't *have* to be this way. If you are lucky your employer will sort out the details of healthcare and health insurance for you and your family. If you have any say in this matter, you should try to get a firm commitment to full-coverage healthcare as part of your remuneration package. This sort of benefit is typical for people coming to Chicago for high-profile executive positions. People coming as full-time students will probably also be able to take advantage of a health plan connected with their school. For those not fortunate enough to have this important matter taken care of, a brief overview of the U.S. healthcare system and your options for the best and most economical healthcare as a newcomer to Chicago are provided here.

U.S. Healthcare: Who Pays and Who Benefits

Few topics in American life excite the natives more than healthcare, and these days, few people have anything good to say about it. You have to understand that the complaining is all relative; most Americans who had to spend a week under the healthcare systems available to most of the world's population would come running back home. The majority of Americans today have experienced no healthcare system other than the one they've got, and they have seen it become more and more expensive over the years, while the quality of care declines markedly. This is the main source of grievance. Today neither doctors, healthcare workers, nor patients are happy with the healthcare system; only investors are, because it is a huge profit-making industry. Unfortunately it seems to have lost sight of the patient's welfare. Attempts on the part of the government to impose reform on the healthcare industry have failed because too many powerful interests stand to lose if the cost of healthcare is reduced, or the quality of it improved, for ordinary people.

Getting Healthcare

Following is a brief primer about healthcare options in Chicago. Terms from healthcare jargon—mastery of which is nearly mandatory if you want to commiserate about your health with Americans—are highlighted.

Though it is possible to take care of your health on a "pay as you go" basis, nobody who could afford to do this actually would. It is so unusual that the healthcare delivery system has virtually no provision for it. Most people get health insurance in one of two basic forms, by belonging to an **HMO** (Health Maintenance Organization, discussed below) or a **PPO** (Preferred Provider Organization). A PPO is closer in spirit to old-fashioned **indemnity health insurance** in which you pay a **premium,** typically monthly or four times a year, and in exchange the insurance company reimburses your doctor, hospitals, medical testing facilities, and the like. The insurance company provides you with a list of preferred **providers** (a doctor or anybody else that provides care, therapy, or diagnostic services). When you use these providers the insurance company pays most or all of your expenses, but if you use other providers (if you are traveling, for example) your out-of-pocket expenses may be higher. **Out-of-pocket expenses** is the term used for any money that you have to pay toward your healthcare in addition to the premiums that you pay for insurance or HMO membership.

Before this arrangement of healthcare reimbursement starts working, however, you will have to spend your own money on healthcare until you have spent up to your **deductible**, an amount of money you agree to pay on your own, per year, before insurance becomes effective. The higher deductible you choose, the lower your insurance premiums. Once you have spent this amount of money within a single year, insurance will pay for either all or a percentage of covered healthcare costs, depending on the individual plan. When the insurance company pays part of a medical expense and you pay for the rest, this is referred to as **copayment**. For example, the insurance company may pay 80 percent, and you pay 20 percent, until your expenses reach a certain agreed-upon figure, after which insurance typically pays for everything, again up to a specified limit.

There are any number of conditions, treatments, and other health-related expenses that insurance will not pay for. These are spelled out in detail in any policy documents or prospectuses of insurance companies. First for consideration among these is a **pre-existing condition**, a medical condition requiring treatment, drugs, or the like that you had at the time you applied for insurance. Normally insurance companies will not assume responsibility for these, which seems to fly in the face of the notion of healthcare, but there it is. There is also a very large class of procedures and treatments that your insurance company may pay for, but only if they are approved for coverage *before* you get them. So don't assume that anything that your doctor wants to do or recommends that you do will be paid for by your insurance. If you are in any doubt at all, consult your insurance company first.

HMOs came to life in the 1970s and were touted as the answer to all that was wrong with health insurance. Today, however, they are the object of much scorn among the general public, mainly because of the way they are managed. Under an HMO, you pay a membership fee that entitles you to use the healthcare services of the HMO, as deemed necessary by the HMO. When you belong to an HMO, your main doctor is either employed by or has a contractual relationship with the HMO; so your doctor

110

gets paid not on the basis of what he does for you but on the basis of his agreement with the HMO. Under an HMO you generally have less choice about who and what facilities you use for your healthcare—decisions about that are made by the HMO administrators—but you will also probably have fewer out-of-pocket expenses than you would have with health insurance. Other things being equal (which they are not), membership in an HMO is generally more expensive than membership in a PPO, or than ordinary indemnity health insurance.

Whether you join an HMO, a PPO, or take out ordinary health insurance, your point of contact with the healthcare system is your **primary care physician (PCP)**, who is typically a family practitioner (more or less the equivalent of a G.P., or general practitioner) or an internist and who carries the title **M.D.** (doctor of medicine) or **D.O.** (doctor of osteopathy, a degree conferred by a school of osteopathic medicine, which trains doctors in the usual ways of Western medicine in addition to specific training in osteopathic manipulation). Your PCP will elect to either handle your healthcare concern, or will refer you to a specialist.

In recent years the concept of **managed care** has emerged and has become the main bugbear of healthcare users in the United States. From the point of view of healthcare administrators, managed care is "a prepaid health plan or insurance program where beneficiaries receive medical services in a coordinated manner so as to eliminate unnecessary medical services." From the patient's point of view, managed care is the system by which healthcare providers can avoid giving care as a way of saving money and maximizing profits. The withholding of care, or unwillingness to pay for care perceived to be needed by the patient, is the main complaint about managed care among ordinary people. The second most common complaint about managed care is the Byzantine bureaucracy that accompanies its implementation and that very often leaves the patient reeling in confusion.

111

There is at present no general government-sponsored health-care system in the United States, but two programs cover certain categories of patients. **Medicaid** provides healthcare for people living in poverty. To qualify for Medicaid you have to be demon-strably indigent. Unless you are already on some kind of govern-ment benefit, you will not qualify for the program, which in any case provides probably the worst and least desirable healthcare available. About the only group of foreign residents in Chicago who may qualify for some Medicaid benefits are refugees and asy-lum seekers. **Medicare** is a federally sponsored program that pro-vides certain healthcare benefits to people over age 65, and to the blind, disabled, and people with renal (kidney) disease. Medicare operates like insurance; beneficiaries pay deductibles, premiums, and copayments in order to receive services.

Getting a Doctor

Once you have sorted out your healthcare provision (and it makes sense to do this first), settle on a doctor. If you join an HMO, you will be assigned to a doctor or to a doctor's office; with health insurance or a PPO, you may be given a list of independent doctors to choose from. If you have the opportunity, try to get a personal recommendation from somebody who has a good doctor. If this isn't possible, try a doctor recommended to you by your insurance company. You have the right to be satisfied with your doctor, and you shouldn't hesitate to keep looking until you find one that you like. Healthcare is an expensive consumer service in the United States, and there is no reason that you shouldn't be completely comfortable with your family doctor and satisfied that you are getting value for your money. You should be able to find either a male or female doctor if you have a preference, and with the great number of foreign doctors who work in Chicagoland, you can probably find someone of your own nationality if you wish, or a doctor who speaks a language other than English that you are more comfortable with.

Tips for the Health Consumer

Many people make their living matching up people who need insurance with those who provide it. Once these people find out about you, you may know no rest until one of them has succeeded in selling you a plan. For this reason, you are wise to educate yourself thoroughly about healthcare options *before* you start shopping around for a plan. Read and compare the literature about health insurance plans available from insurance agents or companies. Avoid the fatal step of letting an insurance agent visit you at home. He won't want to leave until he's sold you something. When you have evaluated a number of plans and settled on one that suits your needs, fill out the (lengthy) application and only then begin to deal directly with an agent or company representative.

If you or a family member suffers from any chronic or ongoing condition it is especially important that you bring documentation about it, in English if possible, with you. This should include any "work-up" notes your doctor has and information about any prescription medicines you take or have taken regularly.

Dental Care and Insurance

Most health insurance policies and plans have optional provision for dental care; an additional premium is payable. If you have children, or if you have a history of teeth that need costly repairs regularly, it is worth your while to have dental insurance coverage. If you have good teeth that rarely need much more than cleaning and looking over, it is probably more economical to pay your dentist out of pocket once or twice a year when you visit.

Try first to find a dentist on somebody's recommendation; if this doesn't work, you can try the Yellow Pages. Properly qualified dentists should have D.M.D. or D.D.S. after their name. Practitioners of various other dental arts and crafts use the term "dentist" but in fact have no justifiable claim to put their fingers in your mouth.

113

Eyecare and Eyewear

Most health insurance plans offer a rider that covers yearly eye exams with a small copayment, plus a discount on new glasses or contact lenses. If you wear corrective lenses, it is usually economical to have such a plan; without one, a full vision examination will cost at least $50.

You can get your eyes tested and choose lenses or glasses all in one place, but you can also simply get a prescription from an optician, optometrist, or ophthalmologist and have it filled at one of the businesses, such as **Lenscrafters**, that make up eyeglasses and contact lenses on the spot. This is usually faster and cheaper.

Alternative Medicine and Therapies

Chicago is the headquarters of the American Medical Association, the American Hospital Association, the American Dental Association, and the American College of Surgeons, and thus a very bastion of the technology driven, high-cost, high-intervention healthcare that is today associated with Western medicine. It is also home to the country's largest medical school (at the University of Illinois), as well as two highly prestigious medical schools, those connected with Northwestern University and the University of Chicago. You might then expect to find very little in the way of gentler, more traditional approaches to health and healing. Fortunately that picture is changing as people becoming increasingly skeptical about and disillusioned with the high cost and ineffectiveness of allopathic medicine, which is essentially what is available from the mainstream healthcare system.

A movement away from conventional (and expensive) Western allopathic medicine is evident everywhere in the West today. By doing a little footwork you can find practitioners of all the better-known alternative therapies (homeopathy, herbal medicine, Ayurveda, acupuncture, and a great number of -ologies) in the Chicago area. In general these therapies are less expensive than conventional medicine, but you should know from the outset that health insurance will not pay for any of them. Inquire first in your community where to look for such therapies. You can also consult the Yellow Pages under the following headings:

- acupuncture
- chiropractic physicians
- herbs
- holistic practitioners
- naprapaths
- naturopaths
- pharmacies — homeopathic
- reflexologists

BEING STREETWISE IN CHICAGO

American cities suffer a dreadful reputation abroad with regard to personal safety, thanks mostly to the sensationalism of Hollywood. It should come as a relief to you to know that the vast majority of Chicagoans pass their days, weeks, and months with very little likelihood that they will be the victim of a violent crime. At the same time, however, the resident of Chicago has to realize that here, as in many American cities, an appreciable percentage of people own guns, and that there are street gangs and others involved in the drug trade.

Many families choose to live in the suburbs for this reason, forsaking whatever cultural advantages the city offers for the security of a relatively crime-free environment. But even in the city of Chicago, the crimes that create the statistics are much more localized than you would guess. The vast majority of crime in Chicago is perpetrated by poor blacks against other poor blacks, in poor black neighborhoods. If you are fortunate enough to be able to steer clear of these high crime areas and observe other sensible precautions, you should not have to spend any time worrying about your or your family's personal safety.

Safety at Home

No matter where you live in Chicagoland, there is the possibility that your house may be burglarized, or "burgled," as Americans say. There are a number of ways to minimize the possibility of this happening to you. The most effective deterrent to burglars is the obvious presence of someone in the home. If you have the opportunity to work from home, or if you have a stay-at-home spouse, you have probably nipped the problem in the bud. If your house is empty for large parts of the day, especially in the winter months when darkness falls early, you should consider any of the following:

- Install a burglar alarm or security system. This is probably necessary only if you live in an area prone to frequent burglaries, or if your insurance company requires that you do so because of the nature of what you keep in the house.
- Join a Neighborhood Watch scheme. These organizations are free and a very effective deterrent to crime for entire neighborhoods. It is the modern, formalized version of what used to take place naturally and was taken for granted: people who live in a local area watch out for each other and take note of anything that looks suspicious.
- Do a "security audit" of your house. Check all vulnerable points of entry and take measures to strengthen your defenses. You might consider, for example, bars or a grate for ground level windows, a security fence, and secure locks for all windows and doors. Trees and shrubs may provide atmosphere and privacy for your home, but if they shield the view of it from the road or from other neighbors, they also create good cover for burglars.
- Set one or more lights in your house on timer switches to go on and off in something that simulates a natural pattern. Such timers are inexpensive and available from hardware stores or discount centers.

When you are at home there is very little need to worry about security. Keep in mind that there is no access to your house easier than one that you permit to happen; so keep your doors locked and exercise a skeptical curiosity about any strangers who call unexpectedly. All tradespeople, especially those who work for utilities such as the gas company and phone company, are uniformed, drive easily identifiable vehicles, and carry picture identification, which they should not hesitate to show you.

Safety on the Street

If you have lived in, worked in, or visited any of the world's large cities, chances are that you are already familiar with the sensible precautions that people take to maximize their personal safety. There are no special rules that apply to Chicago. You will be safe when walking, driving, or using public transportation under all normal circumstances. The times and situations that you should either avoid or approach with caution are given below. Everything applies in double measure to women or children alone, who are perhaps the most vulnerable to opportune crimes.

Public transportation is safe during the hours that you are most likely to be out: up to 9 p.m. during the week, and later on weekends, when people are returning home from entertainment outings. Outside of these times, buses tend to be safe, although the people who ride them become less and less savory as the night wears on. It is sensible for women traveling alone to avoid subways and Ls after 10 p.m.; there may be long waits on deserted platforms that provide an opportunity for unwanted attention from men who have nothing better to do. Because of the city's racial divisions, white people tend to avoid the Ls and subways that pass mainly through black neighborhoods after the evening rush hour. These include the Green Line in its entirety, the Red Line south of the Loop, and the Blue Line west (but not northwest) of the Loop. The Ls going to the North Side generally feel

117

safe until late at night. After midnight, when service is only provided at half-hour intervals on CTA trains, all of them are best avoided unless you can effect a Rambo-like aura.

Again owing to the city's racial divisions, there are many areas of the city where white people almost never appear on the street by night or day. If you are other than black, there is very little likelihood that you would even have a reason to go to these areas, except perhaps to drive through on the way to somewhere else. The areas generally avoided by all except the black population are

- the South Side, on either side of the Dan Ryan Expressway to 95th Street. The black area extends about two miles east and west of the expressway and many of the city's poorest and most crime-ridden housing projects are in this area. But note that there are many areas within this large expanse that are relatively safe, such as Bridgeport, Hyde Park, and Chinatown.
- the West Side, on either side of the Eisenhower Expressway to Austin Avenue. The black area extends about two miles north and south of the expressway, slowly melding to Latino areas in several places.

Cheerful riders on the Green Line.

Black people who appear in otherwise "all-white" areas of the city may experience a hostile, although not usually a violent or threatening reception. Though housing is still fairly segregated, the workforce is everywhere made up of people of all different backgrounds, so the presence of people of color in any part of Chicagoland is not remarkable during working hours. The places where racial tensions have occasionally erupted into violence in recent times is in "border" neighborhoods where a working-class white neighborhood borders an expanding black area, such as in Bridgeport on the southwest side or west suburban Cicero.

Drug Use and Abuse

The only two legal and minimally controlled drugs in the United States are alcohol and tobacco. The social use of alcohol is discussed in Chapter 10, and smoking is touched on in Chapters 9 and 10. Alcohol is not sold to people under the age of 21, and cigarettes are not sold to children under 18. Nevertheless, young people under these legal ages seem to find little difficulty in procuring these "adult" substances. If you are a parent of high school-aged children who attend public schools, it is probably wise to prepare yourself for these drugs to make some appearance in the lives of your children or your children's friends.

People in countries around the world probably hear the very worst aspects of the illegal drug problem in U.S. cities. This is not to say that the problem is not very real and serious, but you may be relieved to find that the use of drugs such as cocaine, crack, heroin, and even marijuana is unheard of in most social circles and would be seriously frowned on if not actually reported to the police. Illegal drug use is largely a phenomenon of the young (certainly including college-age students) and the poor. Adults who a generation ago may have used some recreational drugs quite freely, today's "baby boomers," now for the most part frown on their use as much as their parents did before them. It is unlikely that you will encounter any illegal drug use whatever in people over the

119

age of about 30; for some people younger than this, marijuana, though illegal, is a popular recreational drug.

Many Americans develop habituation or dependency problems with prescription drugs, such as sedatives, barbiturates, "diet pills" that may contain amphetamines, painkillers, and antidepressant drugs. This is due to many different factors, certainly including the tendency of doctors to treat symptoms rather than causes, and the *idée fixe* of both American doctors and patients that a successful consultation ends with the issuing of a prescription for an expensive drug. You should be very careful to discuss with your doctor the reason for any medicines that he or she prescribes. Try to be sure that any suggested drug regimen has a short-term goal in view, after which the drug will no longer be needed.

DEALING WITH EMERGENCIES

Emergency services (the police, fire department, or an ambulance) can be reached from any telephone by dialing 911. This is standard throughout the United States, but not the same as the 999 that is used in Europe and some other places. If you dial 911 (which you should only do in a *real* emergency), be prepared to give your name and tell where you are; the operator can usually determine what telephone number you are calling from.

Chapter Six

TASTING CHICAGO

I give you Chicago. It is not London and Harvard. It is not Paris and buttermilk. It is American in every chitling and sparerib. It is alive from snout to tail.

—H.L. Mencken

FOOD FOR YOUR TABLE

Chicago offers the consumer a very wide range of options for stocking the larder. You shouldn't have trouble finding all the ingredients for the things you liked to cook at home, as well as the ingredients for things that Americans cook (or very often, warm up in their microwaves). If you require foods that are used in the most popular cuisines (Italian, Mexican, and ordinary American), you will find them in the local supermarket. More specialized, exotic, and imported ingredients can be found in specialty shops all over Chicago but mostly concentrated in the neighborhoods of foreigners who share the same palate. If you're not interested in

121

the ingredients but only in the finished product, you can probably also find a delicatessen or restaurant that serves the dish of your dreams already made up and ready to carry away. We'll begin our survey of food shopping at the most general, bland end of the market and work our way down to exotic particulars.

As everywhere in America, shopping in Chicago supermarkets is the path of least resistance. American supermarkets in recent years have become quite homogenous to the point that you almost know what one will look like inside before you go in. The range of products carried and their arrangement is the result of many years of market analysis, the aim of which is to make your visit to the supermarket easy for you, and profitable for it. A very large percentage of space in supermarkets is devoted to ready-made foods, quick mixes, and frozen foods that only need warming up. The target consumer of these foods is the busy urbanite who has little time to cook (or perhaps doesn't really know how) but wants to be able to put something tasty, or at least tasty-looking, on the table.

Warm foods for those cold winter nights on North Clark Street.

For this reason, you may feel initially bewildered in the supermarket, being surrounded by food but seeing nothing that you actually came to buy or that you want to eat. This will be particularly true if you are used to buying your food in places where you can actually see what it is before you take it home. Nearly all supermarket food is prepackaged, with its actual appearance concealed behind very attractive, and often deceptive photographs. In addition to this there is a sort of "grammar" of food packaging in America that, once you've mastered it, is useful shorthand for recognizing products by the shape, color, and design of the packaging. But until you get the hang of this, you will have to do a lot of reading of labels. It is no deficit in your perceptive abilities that makes you feel lost in the supermarket, you simply have to learn to "read" the place in order to move about efficiently to find the things you need. Unfortunately no textbook is available; mastery comes with practice.

There are two main supermarket chains in Chicagoland, **Jewel** and **Dominick's**, both offering the same wide variety of prepared foods, in addition to fresh produce, fish, meat, and dairy products. Both chains are owned by even larger chains of supermarkets. Two convenience store chains that are nearly ubiquitous merit mention here as well: **White Hen Pantry** and **7-11.** Outlets of these are normally open 24 hours and offer a smaller and more expensive selection of the foods you are most likely to run out of or crave suddenly. A third and smaller supermarket chain, **Treasure Island**, has only five supermarkets, all on the north and near north sides, but they offer a far wider selection of international foods than the two giants; the genuine foodie will not want to shop anywhere else, save the specialty food shops.

Supermarkets that place an emphasis on whole foods and organic produce are **Fresh Fields** (on Elston Avenue and in Evanston) and **Whole Foods** (North and Sheffield). Finally, a relative new chain, **Delray Farms**, with a handful of Chicago locations, offers what is probably the closest thing to an Old World shopping experience: fresh produce, meat, milk, and a smaller selection of processed foods in an open atmosphere.

You Say Tomato …

There is quite a lot of variety in terms for food even within the United States, so it is very likely that the variety of English you know uses a word different from the one Chicagoans use for some kind of food. Here is a table, by no means exhaustive, of the commonest differences:

American word	other English word
beet	beetroot
bok choi	Chinese leaves
candy	sweets
chicory	endive
cilantro	coriander
cookie	biscuit (sweetened)
corn	maize
cornstarch	corn flour
cracker	biscuit (unsweetened)
daikon	white radish
dessert	pudding
eggplant	aubergine
french fries	chips
golden raisins	sultanas
ground beef, hamburger	mince
ham	gammon
Jell-O	jelly
legumes (i.e., beans)	pulses
okra	ladies' fingers
pasta flour	semolina

peanut	groundnut
persimmon	sharon fruit
popsicle	ice lolly
potato chips	crisps
powdered sugar	icing sugar
rutabaga	swede
sausages	bangers
scallion, green onion	spring onion
shrimp	prawns
snow peas	mangetout
soda, pop, soda pop	fizzy drink
summer squash	marrow
tangerine	clementine
winter squash	pumpkin
zucchini	courgette

Food Labeling

There are two sorts of food labeling that you should educate yourself about. The important one is the official, legally mandated food label that appears on all food products sold, and that always carries the heading **Nutrition Facts**. It is a very useful and informative tool for telling you what is in food and what its nutrient value is. Somewhere near the Nutrition Facts table you will also find a list that begins with the word "Ingredients." This tells you all the things that the food product contains, in descending order of quantity; that is, the ingredient listed first is the main one. The other kind of food labeling is that driven by market forces. It places undue emphasis on the qualities of a food product that are thought likely to appeal to you (such as "low fat," "no sodium," or "all natural ingredients" but ignores other unattractive qualities: that it consists almost entirely of sugar, that it contains nothing that your body actually requires, or that it is extremely high in

125

cholesterol, for example. Study and learn the format of the Nutrition Facts label so that you can absorb its information efficiently; ignore everything else. You only have to look at the average American on the street to know that there is something considerably unbalanced in the general diet. Well over half of Americans are overweight, from a combination of eating too many foods too high in fat and sugar, and getting too little exercise.

Beverage Basics

Chicago and many surrounding suburbs get their drinking **water** from Lake Michigan. Pumping stations that bring the water to treatment facilities can be seen from the shoreline. As big city water goes it is not terrible, but it carries aromatic vestiges of its fishy origins and its treatment in the chlorination plant. Most of the taste can be removed by using a water filtering system, either one with a replaceable filter in a pitcher or one that is attached to your kitchen tap. Several suburbs buy their water from the city of Chicago and drink the very same lake water. Municipalities with water that comes from somewhere other than Lake Michigan generally have even worse-tasting well water that requires softening treatment. Consult with people in the area where you live to learn more specific details about the local water. Tap water in all cases is safe to drink, even if not very palatable. Better tasting water is available bottled in all food stores; there is a wide variety of North American and European waters to choose from.

Because of the American obsession with monitoring the consumption of fat, **milk** is sold in several varieties that have varying amounts of fat removed. Terminology for these is evolving but seems to be moving toward a system of identifying varieties of milk by the percentage of fat they contain. There is fat-free milk, 1 percent milk (formerly called skim milk), 2 percent milk (sometimes called low-fat milk and perhaps the most widely used variety), and finally whole milk, with none of the fat taken out. The names for various products that contain cream may also be different from what you're used to. A popular product called **half and half** — half milk, half cream — is added to coffee and sometimes tea. Other varieties are light cream, whipping cream, which contains enough fat that it will become stiff when whipped, and heavy cream, used in cooking.

Americans usually use **ice** in cold drinks, both winter and summer. Everyone makes and keeps ice cubes in their home freezers, and many refrigerators come with an internal ice-cube making facility. If you want a cold drink without ice you should ask for it that way.

Good quality **coffee and tea** are available in Chicago, but you should never expect them as a matter of course. The default versions of these beverages, that is the ones served in ordinary American restaurants and often in people's homes, are likely to be a far cry from what you think of as a good cup. The cup of coffee you get in an ordinary Chicago restaurant, such as a diner or a fast food outlet, is weak, acrid, of the cheapest quality, and best avoided. Nevertheless, appreciation for good quality coffee is ever increasing in American cities and it is now easier to find, for example in any of the various "coffee bars," such as Starbucks, and in any restaurant that has even the slightest European or high-tone pretensions. Every coffee-serving establishment also serves decaffeinated coffee, or "decaf."

The appreciation of good quality tea is still very much in its infancy in Chicago. Loose tea is not to be had in either supermarkets or most restaurants, which sell or use only teabags. You will have to go to a tea and coffee specialty shop (there is at least one in every upscale neighborhood), or to an Asian or Indian food store. Americans drink tea more often with lemon than with milk, and teas sold in teabags tend to be fairly weak on account of this. **Iced tea** is a popular American beverage, particularly in the summer; it is served with lemon and sometimes sugar. When you order hot tea in a restaurant, don't be surprised to see a pot of moderately hot water with a teabag beside it arrive at your table. You do the brewing yourself.

Fruit juices and other drinks based on them are popular with people of all ages. Many of these consist almost entirely of sugar, water, and coloring; you should read the nutrition label to learn how much fruit juice is actually used. A popular and economical way to buy fruit juices is in the form of **frozen concentrate**; you buy a can that you then mix with three parts water in a pitcher.

Alcoholic beverages are sold widely in the Chicago area in supermarkets and in liquor stores. You must be 21 years old to buy any beverages containing alcohol. A vendor in doubt about someone's having attained this age is likely to ask for a driver's license as proof of age and identity.

EATING, CHICAGO STYLE

While it is probably not necessary to make major changes in the way you prepare food if you don't want to—ingredients can probably be found for most of the things you cook, though some of them might take some searching for—at some point you will probably want to try some American recipes. There isn't a fully-fledged cuisine associated with Chicago or with the Midwest, the food tends to be fairly mainstream American in this part of the country. Recipes for dishes that might be called real Chicago food are as likely to appear in the food section of daily Chicago papers as anywhere else.

A handful of foods are associated with Chicago, to the point that they earn the epithet "Chicago-style" when served in other parts of the country. You may want to try them eventually to feel that you are a true Chicagoan, but be warned, they are not foods for the faint of heart and each packs a wallop of calories, cholesterol, or both! Here are the main contenders for the archetypal Chicago dish, along with a few places to sample them:

- **Barbecued Ribs:** These are popular all over the United States but have an avid following in Chicago. Carson's, with two locations in Chicagoland, is certainly the most hyped rib restaurant and serves a good plateful. For a really authentic and unpretentious rib feast off the beaten track, try Biasetti's Steak & Rib House on Irving Park near Ashland. And if you just want to take them home and savor them in private, Ribs & Bibs at 53rd and Dorchester should do the trick.
- **Deep-dish Pizza:** It's the food that made Chicago famous and is responsible for spinning off restaurant franchises in far-flung corners of the globe. It's easy to find: the main franchise restaurants, Giordano's, Edwardo's, and Pizzeria Uno, all serve up good representative pies. You will probably discover your own neighborhood favorites if you go in for this sort of thing.
- **Italian Beef:** There is probably nothing like it in Italy: thinly sliced beef cooked in juice and Italian spices and served on a roll. The two outlets that are generally considered to be a cut above the others are Al's on Taylor near Sheffield and Mr. Beef on Orleans near Huron.

- **Hot Dogs:** It's hard to believe that people could be rabidly enthusiastic about a food that is nearly universally available and whose ingredients have always been something of a mystery. But that's Chicago. Hot dog stands are everywhere to be found, but three attract people from hundreds of miles away, believe it or not: Fluky's in Lincolnwood, on Touhy just west of Kedzie; Gene & Jude's on River Road in River Grove; and the cheekily named Wiener's Circle, on Clark just north of Wrightwood (pictured below).

  If you notice the preponderance of red meat here, remember that Chicago was once the "hog butcher of the world," and operated the world's biggest stockyards for 100 years!

A hotdog stand, home of simple but fabled food.

If you want to delve more deeply into American cooking, there are a number of well-developed regional cuisines, with numerous cookbooks devoted to each of them. For general purpose American cookbooks, two stand out: **Joy of Cooking**, and the **Fanny Farmer Cookbook**. Each is published in a new, updated edition every few years. Most people agree that the newer editions have sacrificed a lot of taste and richness in food for concerns about cooking healthier food. For more traditional recipes, you might want to pick up a used edition of either of these books in a used bookstore, rather than buy the current edition new. Both new and old editions are widely available.

If you plan to do any American-style cooking at all, the best advice is to adopt the American system of measurement from the start. While it is possible to convert American recipes to metric equivalents, and all good cookbooks have conversion tables, the fact is that by the time you do this, you could well have put an entire dish together. The American system of measurement is quick and easy. It uses measuring devices that are cheap and widely available. A kitchen scale is not required unless you want to enter the high end of cooking. Invest in a set of measuring cups ($1/4$, $1/3$, $1/2$, and 1 cup containers) and a set of measuring spoons ($1/4$, $1/2$, and 1 teaspoon, plus $1/2$ and 1 tablespoon measures). These are the usual measurements you will see in American recipes. You can study the tables in any cookbook to learn the equivalents of all these measurements and their relationships to each other; if you use them frequently, they will soon become second nature.

If you have used the British Imperial system of measurement, be warned that some units with the same name are *not* equivalent: a British pint is 4 ounces larger than an American pint; the corresponding measures of British quarts and gallons (in fact rarely used in Britain anyway) are proportionally larger. A U.S. pint contains 16 ounces, and is the equivalent of 2 cups, a cup containing 8 ounces. A British pint contains 20 ounces.

The Meal Plan

The traditional three meals a day is what most Chicagoans eat, though it must be said that people's eating habits are very individualistic and you can eat more or less what you want when you want without being thought strange. All meals, unless they are organized as part of a social event or are part of a holiday celebration, tend to be quick and informal, in keeping with the habit of urban Americans to always be in a hurry. **Breakfast** is typically a rushed bite or two before work, or is eaten at work in the first few minutes. Cereal, yogurt, and various kinds of toasted bread are all popular. A more substantial breakfast might include pancakes or eggs, potatoes, and meat, either pork sausage or bacon. Many restaurants offer breakfast specials at very reasonable prices. It is not unusual for people to meet in a restaurant for a social breakfast, especially if they cannot find any other convenient time for getting together. **Lunch** is eaten from noon onward; anything after two o'clock would be considered a late lunch. It also tends to be a fairly light meal, especially for people who work and take only half an hour or less to eat. A sandwich or some other form of fast food is typical. Restaurants generally offer a cheaper menu at lunchtime than in the evening, though they often serve the same dishes at both times. **Dinner** (sometimes called supper, especially if eaten at home) is usually the main meal of the day, eaten anywhere from six o'clock onward; eating after nine o'clock would be considered late by most Chicagoans.

On Sundays people often have a substantial meal in the late morning that takes the place of breakfast and lunch and is called **brunch**. Many restaurants offer special brunch menus, typically consisting of an "all-you-can eat" buffet. Brunch in someone's home is a fairly common social affair.

Eating Out

Except for the most fashionable and expensive restaurants, it is not usually necessary to reserve a table in advance at Chicago's restaurants on weekdays. To avoid disappointment on the weekends, a call ahead to secure your place is a good idea. There are two annual restaurant guides published, *Marcellinus Chicago Restaurant Report* and *Zagat Survey of Chicago Restaurants*. Neither is particularly recommended; you will do better to check any of the many other sources of information about restaurants. The daily and weekly press, *Chicago Magazine*, the Internet, and your friends and neighbors will probably provide the best and most up-to-date information about where and where not to eat. All restaurants are required by law to offer smoking and nonsmoking areas; nonsmoking areas are usually the most desirable seating. More than half the restaurants have a liquor license to serve drinks as well as meals. Those that do not have a license usually permit you to bring your own wine or beer to the meal if you wish.

The amount of food served in American restaurants for a single meal is extraordinary and almost vulgar. If you operate on the philosophy that you should always clean your plate, you will become obese in very little time (as many Americans do!). The size of restaurant servings, and of dinner plates, has been growing for years and there seems to be no end in sight. But you will notice that many people take home food that is left on their plates.

This is such standard practice that all restaurants have facilities for dealing with it. Restaurants will provide a container, sometimes called a "doggy bag," and some will even bring you the container so that you can fill it yourself. Many people who live alone or who are too busy to cook eat in restaurants with the knowledge that they will get enough food for at least one if not two extra meals from the experience. If you don't want the food to go to waste, you might as well adopt the custom too.

The Interrogation

In popular restaurants it is now fashionable for waitstaff (a collective term covering waiters and waitresses) to be quite informal and friendly. They may introduce themselves to you by their first names. Perhaps this is because it will soon be necessary for them to engage you in lengthy conversation, during which you must specify your choices about various food options. It is not enough to simply choose from the menu, you then have to go through a list of questions. The philosophy of this system is that everyone can get exactly what they want in the way of food. The serenity of the dining experience has been sacrificed to this. To help you through it, here are the standard options: if you order a salad (always served before the meal, not with or after), you have to choose a salad dressing. Your waitperson will rattle these off for you, but the standard choices are **blue cheese** (usually a mayonnaise-based dressing), **Thousand Island** (a thick orange-colored sauce with unidentified chunks in it), **ranch** (buttermilk and herbs are the foundation), and **Italian** (usually a vinaigrette). If you order beef, you have to specify how it should be cooked (rare, medium, well-done, or some gradation in between). If potatoes come with your meal, you often have a choice between baked, mashed, or french fries. Baked can be served with sour cream or butter or both. And so forth. Americans are used to this question-and-answer period with the server and some take it very seriously; you will get used to it.

Food Delivery

Many restaurants offer a delivery service in their local area. Over a certain specified minimum, there is usually no delivery charge. You can call in your order and expect it to be delivered in less than an hour. Portions are usually of the same generous size that would be served in the restaurant, so you can often get more than one meal out of a food delivery. Menus from various restaurants can be picked up at the restaurants and are sometimes distributed to apartment buildings.

Specialty and Ethnic Foods

If you've exhausted the shelves of your supermarket without finding the ingredients you crave, try visiting some of the areas and stores listed here to find specialty foods from different places around the world. In addition to the food, you will be able to enjoy the flavor of some of Chicago's many ethnic enclaves.

Chinese: Small shops can be found in many different areas of the city, but if you want it all in one place and will accept no substitutes, go to Chinatown on Cermak Road (main shopping street: Wentworth) or Argyle Street (5000 N) between Sheridan and Racine.

German: The German influence on Chicago is at the bedrock level, and the influence of German cuisine has been assimilated into the mainstream of American food. But for the pure experience, try Kuhn's Delicatessen, 3053 N. Lincoln Ave, as well as its two suburban locations. For German pastries that rival those of the Bavarian pastry belt, Lutz Continental Café, near Montrose and Western, is recommended.

Greek: There are a few bakeries and food shops in Greektown, the area around Halsted Street between Van Buren and Madison. Farther afield there is Sparta Grocery near Diversey and Austin.

135

Indian: The best concentration of shops and restaurants is on Devon Avenue between Western and California.

Italian: All supermarkets carry most of what you would want in the way of Italian food, which is popular with all Americans. For a more authentic flavor, try Taylor Street (1000 S) on the Near West Side, between Racine and Southport.

Japanese: Star Market, 3349 N. Clark, is the best in-town bet.

Korean: Try Lawrence Avenue between Kedzie and Pulaski where the smell of the kimchi comes out to greet you.

Mexican: Owing to its popularity with Chicagoans, a fairly wide range of Mexican foods can be found in all supermarkets, with the branches in Hispanic neighborhoods offering an even deeper selection. If you want the food buying experience to be totally authentic and prefer to do it in Spanish, try the supermercados in Logan Square, Humboldt Park, Little Village, or Pilsen.

Food with a Latin American flavor on North Milwaukee Avenue.

Middle Eastern: The many different nationalities lumped under this term occupy diverse corners of Chicago, but there is a certain similarity in their cuisines and the various nationals themselves cross over a lot to do the food shopping. There are a couple of shops on W. 63rd Street between Sacramento and Central Park, and another scattering on Clark Street from Montrose northward.

Polish: Milwaukee Avenue and parts of adjacent streets from about Diversey to Addison are a smorgasbord of Polish restaurants, shops, and delicatessens. Good shops in which to find nearly all edible delicacies are Rich's Deli and the Kurowski Sausage Shop, which share premises at 2976-78 N. Milwaukee Avenue. When Poland was still behind the Iron Curtain, Poles visiting Chicago were shocked to see such an abundance of Polish foods, something they could never find at home.

Swedish: A few shops remain in Andersonville, on Clark Street north of Foster.

Thai: Two big groceries compete, within two blocks of each other, on Broadway between Lawrence and Argyle Street.

Vietnamese: Argyle Street has two grocery stores only steps from each other, Hoa Nam and Viet Hoa.

Special Dietary Requirements

Observers of kosher dietary laws will not have any difficulty finding foods in Chicago; all supermarkets carry a range of kosher foods. Those in neighborhoods and suburbs with large Jewish concentrations (Skokie, Rogers Park, and Hyde Park, for instance) carry even more, and you will also find Jewish delicatessens in these areas with an even wider selection.

For Muslims, halal and zabiha butchers can be found mainly on Devon west of Western—where in fact they are displacing all the Jewish and kosher shops that used to be there! The Black

A zabiha (Muslim) butcher shop in Rogers Park.

Muslim community does not strictly or generally observe traditional Muslim dietary laws.

Drinking Out

Bar, lounge, tavern, inn, saloon, and *pub,* roughly in descending order of popularity, are all terms used for drinking establishments. Statistics show that they are decreasing in number, but you probably won't note any shortage where you live. Some bars cater to a particular clientele, such as "sports bars," which show continuous broadcasts of sporting events. Other bars serve the residents of a particular area, and these usually reflect very closely the economic and class features of that area. The Rush Street area (near North) is known for its many bars featuring music and dancing; this area is the destination of those (mostly young) people who are out on the town. The biggest concentration of gay bars is in Lakeview, but these can be found all over the city, especially on the North Side. The most authentic blues bars, featuring live blues or jazz musicians, are mostly on the South side, though there are several downtown locations as well.

Twenty-one is the minimum age for people to drink in bars; anyone who looks like they might be younger is likely to be "carded," that is, asked to show a driver's license as proof of their age.

CHAPTER SEVEN

SAVING AND SPENDING

Chicago is the finest city in the world for the moderate, natural, average man of affairs in which to live. The New Yorker who says Chicago is a city of no luxuries is one of that constantly growing number who are insatiable in their greed for the softer things in life.
— Gustavus Franklin Swift, founder of Swift & Co., the Chicago meatpacking firm

This chapter is about managing your money the American way, which may require a few adjustments from what you're used to. It is also about spending money, which is exceedingly easy to do in Chicago. To begin with, a brief introduction to American money: no one needs to be told what a dollar (symbol: $) is; units smaller than a dollar are all coins. These go by their names: 1 cent (symbol: ¢) is a penny; 5 cents is a nickel; 10 cents is a dime; 25 cents is a quarter; and 50 cents (not much in circulation these days) is a half-dollar. There are $1 coins, but every attempt to introduce them into circulation has failed—people prefer the $1 bill. Other common denominations for bills are $5, $10, $20 (recently newly designed), $50, and $100 (also newly designed). There are larger bills but they are not used in ordinary transactions; most people have never handled any of them.

Cash is acceptable for most financial transactions, but other forms of payment are preferred in many cases. For that reason it is essential for anyone who wishes to function fully in Chicago's economy to have one or more bank accounts.

PERSONAL BANKING

A checking account is the most common sort of bank account for handling your money; it is a rare Chicagoan who is without one. It comes with the accouterments of a checkbook and an ATM (automatic teller machine) card that enables you to withdraw cash and make deposits and payments at ATM machines. Many ATM cards also function as "debit cards," enabling you to use them as you would a check: money is deducted from your checking account when you use the card to buy something. You can use ATMs associated with your own bank for free. When you use an ATM associated with another bank or banking network there is a fee, typically $1 per transaction. In addition to the charge made by the ATM machine, your own bank may charge you a dollar or more for using an ATM outside its network. Give some thought then to the convenience of free ATM machines before choosing your bank. You'll want to be sure that there are enough free machines for withdrawing money near the places you frequent so that you can avoid going out of your way, or being charged for using another bank's machines.

141

A few details about checks and checking accounts may differ from the system you are used to. Here is what you will find in Chicago and elsewhere in the United States. When you open a checking account you are supplied initially with books of personalized checks. These are generally not free; you will have to pay about $15 for the initial supply, though later you can order replacement checks at a much reduced cost through various companies that advertise widely in newspapers and through direct mail. Typically the checks you have written are returned to you each month along with your bank statement, but banks are now trying to get away from this costly (for them) practice by offering a service under the marketing term "safekeeping." They keep the checks you have written and only send you the statement.

A check that is written payable to you can be deposited in your account, or it can be cashed (that is, converted to cash). Whether you are cashing or depositing the check, you must *endorse* a check that is payable to you (sign it in the space provided on the back of the check). If you are depositing the check, it is good practice to write "for deposit only" under your signature. This ensures that, if the check should fall into the wrong hands, it will not be cashed by a perfect stranger. Do not endorse a check until you are ready to do something with it. In some cases the person cashing or depositing the check for you will want to see you endorse it.

Normally only your own bank will cash checks made out to you, and only if you have enough money in your account to cover the amount of the check. In some cases you may be able to cash a check made out to you at the bank it is drawn on, provided that you have proper identification. Banks in general do not provide any free or courtesy services to people who do not have accounts with them, so you will find your own bank is the best place to handle all money and check transactions.

Currency Exchanges

Throughout Chicago you will notice businesses, typically at or near busy intersections, called Currency Exchanges. The name suggests you might be able to convert currency here, as you would at a *bureau de change*, as it is called in Europe and elsewhere. Don't be deceived! A Currency Exchange is really a kind of poor man's bank that handles various financial affairs for people without bank accounts. You can cash a check there (though usually not a personal check), buy a money order, wire money, buy stamps and CTA tokens, and obtain other services such as faxing, having coins rolled, or getting documents notarized—all for a fee. Currency Exchanges are not recommended for services available through banks, usually at better rates and in more congenial surroundings, but you may find a Currency Exchange convenient if you do not yet have banking facilities in Chicago or the United States, or if you want to complete several transactions in a single stop.

Foreign Exchange

There are several banks and other foreign exchange facilities at O'Hare Airport, in the Loop, and along N. Michigan Avenue for buying and selling foreign currency. Elsewhere in the city they are not so easy to come by, except in a few areas frequented by tourists. You can send money abroad to many countries (about 100) with an International Postal Money order, available at post offices. Most banks can accept and send international wire transfers for a fee, but normally perform this service only for their own customers. If you will be sending or receiving money from abroad frequently, you may want to inquire what facilities your bank has for this.

Foreign banks and banks with a special relationship to a particular foreign country normally have an office located in a neighborhood where immigrants of that country are concentrated. Consult people of your own community to learn what facilities may exist using these banks to transfer money internationally.

143

Other Financial Institutions

While most people handle the majority of their financial affairs through a bank, there are other institutions whose services overlap partly or completely with banks, and these may offer you competitive deals. A **savings and loan association** (**S&L** for short) operates more or less like a bank, but is organized under slightly different rules. Traditionally it operated like a Building Society in the United Kingdom, serving as the main conduit for home mortgages, but now the lines between S&Ls and banks is fuzzier and they offer essentially the same services. A financial crisis among S&Ls in the late 1980s and early 1990s that cost the government huge sums to set right partly gave them a bad name. Many have consequently dropped the full name of "savings and loan association" to avoid its negative connotations. Funds held by S&Ls are as secure as those held by banks. There is no need for alarm about their safety.

Another financial institution favored by many people is a **credit union**. Credit unions are capitalized by their members and are organized as cooperatives; membership in one usually requires you to be a member of some identified group, such as a trade union, employee association, or the like. The advantages of credit unions are that they are often able to make loans at lower than average rates (since they do not operate for profit), and they may enable you to establish credit more easily than you could through a bank. Many credit unions operate in Chicago's ethnic communities and are the most user-friendly way for immigrants to get integrated into the American financial system.

YOUR CREDIT RECORD

One of the more daunting tasks of the new consumer in the United States is to establish a credit record. Globalization notwithstanding, credit information about individuals doesn't customarily cross international borders. Even though you may have a sterling credit history in your own country, you will very likely find that you arrive in the United States as an unknown. And in this case, unknown means unloved. Anywhere you apply for credit you will discover that there is a "Catch 22": you can't get new credit without already having credit established!

While it is certainly possible to operate in the modern economy without the use of credit and credit cards, no one does it who doesn't have to: not having a major credit card is an obstacle to a great number of very ordinary transactions, for example, renting a car, or shopping by telephone or Internet. In some cases you can use credit cards from your own country, but these may not always be easy for retailers to authorize. Therefore, make it an early priority to get a U.S.-based credit card (Visa or MasterCard are the most widely accepted) and start to use it, in order to create a favorable electronic shadow of your buying and paying habits. The bank where you establish your accounts will probably be willing to get you a credit card, even if it starts with a fairly low credit limit. This can act as your entry into the American credit reporting system. You should inquire about this when you first open a bank account. Shop around until you find a bank that will issue you a credit card.

If you use and regularly pay at least the required amount on your credit cards, in very little time you will be receiving offers in the mail almost daily for more credit cards. Many credit cards come with various bonuses attached. For example, you may accumulate frequent flier miles with each credit card purchase, or you may get credit toward the purchase of gasoline or a new car every time you use your credit card. When your credit record is established you can pick and choose from among the offers you receive. Most credit cards are free, but some come with an annual fee. Look seriously at any card that charges an annual fee to decide whether it is worth paying for the privilege of using credit that is offered freely elsewhere.

Your credit record is often indexed by your Social Security number (discussed in chapter 8). Make sure you have an SSN before applying for a credit card; most issuers will require it.

AMERICAN RETAILING

Having now put you in possession of all the necessary information for keeping and saving your money, it remains only to say how to spend it. This will never be a problem. The consumer is king in America, and a wide range of choice in goods from all over the world is available at very reasonable prices. You can hardly do other than to follow the horde and spend, spend, spend, taking advantage of all the things to buy.

There are two schools of thought about shopping in Chicagoland and most people take advantage of both, for different purposes. One school says to shop locally, from your neighborhood merchants, and establish good relationships near where you live, though it may mean paying a higher price for some goods. The other school says migrate to a shopping center or superstore that specializes in the thing you want to buy. There you will have a much wider selection to choose from and probably get a better price to boot. Which shopping style you choose probably depends on your temperament as much as anything, but the migration school has many advantages over the local school and will probably win out altogether eventually, except for small and routine purchases. There are superstores for books, computers, sporting goods, furniture, appliances, and nearly every other thing that you could spend more than $100 on.

American retailers are able to offer so much so cheaply for a number of reasons, the primary one being the vastness of the American market and the ability to manufacture and buy in huge quantities. Competition is fierce in nearly all areas of consumer spending. Retailers are constantly looking for ways to economize, enabling them to sell their goods at cheaper prices. One result of this policy over the past several years has been the near disappearance of anything like a career in retail selling. Jobs that involve dealing directly with customers are largely filled by part-time, semi-retired, or student workers; those who pursue it full-time are likely to be ever hopeful of a move up or out, because these jobs offer little in the way of pay or benefits. The result for the consumer is that sales people often know very little about what they are selling. You can no longer go into a store and expect that anyone there will be able to help you, beyond directing you to the thing that you've come to buy. It will pay you to educate yourself as much as you can about what it is you want to buy, because you can't count on there being anyone in a store who can give you better information than you can find yourself.

Shopping Habits

Retailers and manufacturers alike are passionately devoted to finding ways of parting you from your cash and offer no end of incentives to achieve this. The result in many cases is for the consumer to become consumed in debt, with all credit cards and charge accounts "maxed out" (charged up to the limit of available credit). This is a serious danger for anyone who has not operated before in an economy with easy consumer credit. The new arrival in the

147

Convenience for the consumer society. Drugstores sell household goods, along with dispensing medical prescriptions.

United States may be at an initial advantage in being unable to secure easy credit so quickly, but once your credit is established you should ever be wary of the temptation to acquire goods that you don't have to pay for until far in the future. Though many credit cards offer an attractive introductory rate of interest, most charge a very high rate of interest (15–20 percent), and many Americans get into serious financial trouble through their failure to understand how quickly their indebtedness can grow. A bad credit rating is even worse than no credit rating at all, so be sure that you don't put more on your credit cards than you can pay off.

That said, there are many ways to save a lot in what you spend by taking skillful advantage of the inducements that will constantly be coming your way. You can save 10 percent or more on your food bill by using coupons. These are distributed through newspapers, especially in the big Sunday editions, which normally have booklets full of coupons that can be redeemed for discounts on food and other supermarket items. If you have the patience to clip and organize them, they will more than pay back the cost of the newspaper. A small family can easily save as much as $20 a week by taking advantage of coupons.

For large purchases you may be able to take advantage of an initial interest-free credit period. These deals are usually advertised as "0 percent interest" or "no payments for 6 months" or until some specified date in the future, and are typically associated with computers, furniture, and major appliances such as televisions and refrigerators. The point to understand about these deals is that finance charges (interest on credit you receive) are payable by you *retroactively* for the so-called interest-free period if you do not pay off the entire debt at the end of the "interest-free" period. If you do not pay cash for the entire purchase at the end of the initial period, then you have gained nothing by taking advantage of the deal, and you will be charged steep interest (15 percent or more) until you have paid off the entire debt. Such deals are normally offered only to people who have a satisfactory credit history, so you may not qualify if you are new to the United States.

There is very little haggling for the price of new goods in Chicago. Consumer products are priced competitively and are often discounted or on sale, so it is expected that you will simply pay the price advertised. You should, however, haggle on a few items you can usually get cheaper than the listed price: new and used cars, beds and mattresses, and all used merchandise. If you buy a residential property—house or condo—it is usual to get into a moderately lengthy exercise of give and take on the price, but this is not the case with rent. It is not advisable to try to get rent reduced; you will be viewed immediately as a cheap foreigner!

As much as Americans love to shop, they seem to be equally fond of returning items purchased when they find, on arriving home, that they don't like them any more. Most stores are very understanding about this and will accept returned merchandise with no questions asked, provided of course that the merchandise is undamaged and that you have a sales receipt for it.

Marketing Geography

If you are new to the United States it is useful to know how advertisers and marketers use Americans' knowledge (or ignorance) of the rest of the world to make products seem more attractive. This amounts to learning what Americans' popular associations with various places are. Wherever in the world you come from, you will find some of the notions quaint, but remember, the promotional tactics exist mostly to enhance the consumer's perception of the product and very often have little to do with reality.

The adjective *European* holds a special place in American marketing. You can translate it as "sophisticated," "stylish," "modern," or "cleverly engineered" depending on the product. The concept takes advantage of the fact that while most Americans (75 percent) are of European descent, most have either never been to Europe, or have gone there on some sort of enchanted holiday and so view it as a Shangri-La, a place where everything is better. If you are European yourself, you will recognize this as an obvious con.

Several European countries' names may be used to enhance the perception of certain features of products. French and Italian styling are thought superior, German engineering is respected, and the epithet "Scandinavian" is popular in association with a number of products ranging from skin care to furniture. Poorer or formerly communist European countries don't figure in any of these associations, but the term *Mediterranean* can be used to cast a pleasing aura over certain foods, cosmetics, and clothing.

Taxing Situations

Foreigners shopping in the United States are often shocked to arrive at the cashier and find that the item they picked out suddenly costs more than what is printed on the price tag. This is because **sales tax** is added at the point of sale. Various government authorities have the power to collect sales taxes, and those who can, do. In the city of Chicago the sales tax is a whopping 8.75 percent on most goods; 6.25 percent goes to the state of Illinois and the rest to the city. The total percentage varies in the different suburbs. In Indiana the state sales tax is 5 percent; in Wisconsin it is 5.1 percent. There are a few states left in the United States that don't charge sales tax, but you have to go pretty far afield from Chicago to reach any of them.

Buying on the Cheap

The United States is the consumer society *par excellence* and people go through consumer goods as fast as many cultures go through food. A vast array of second-hand goods are recycled into the consumer market via resale shops (mostly operated by and for charities) and sales advertised as yard or garage sales. Flea markets are in essence collective yard sales, where individuals gather in one place to sell unwanted goods from tables or the back of their cars. In the city, such markets and sales are less common, but they are not hard to find in the suburbs. The main outlets for second-hand consumer and household goods in the city are charity shops, operated by GoodWill Industries, the Salvation Army, and other charitable concerns such as hospitals. Resale shops in better neighborhoods generally have the best selection and quality of goods. A few can be found in wealthier suburbs, and these are treasure-trove for those with high tastes and low budgets.

In the suburbs, garage and yard sales are a time-honored weekend activity; you can hardly drive around in the summertime without coming across two or three. If you are seriously bargain-hunting, go early on the morning of the first day of a sale. You will find a small army of like-minded people looking to snap up the best buys before others arrive. Do not show up at garage or yard sales before the advertised starting time; this will not draw a friendly response from the sellers.

Individuals sell used goods through "want ads" that appear in the newspapers every day. The most popular items sold in this way are furniture, appliances, and cars. If you would rather deal with an individual than a professional seller, you may want to consult the ads for merchandise. There is usually some leeway on the price of anything advertised in this way, but you should be aware that you are not protected by any sort of guarantee.

CHICAGOLAND SHOPPING GUIDE

The ads in a single day's newspaper can give you a pretty good feel for what you can buy in Chicago and at what price. Remember: something is always on sale somewhere. The following notes are to fill in the background of the shopping scene and to help you identify the place that most people would think of for buying particular kinds of goods. Where no phone number or location information is given, consult the Yellow Pages.

Appliances: large appliances such as refrigerators, freezers, stoves, and the like are sold by department stores, home improvement warehouses such as **Home Depot**, and appliance superstores such as **Best Buy.**

Art: The more expensive "establishment" galleries are along North Michigan Avenue. Newer, more experimental and avant-garde items can be admired and purchased in the River North area.

Books: Borders and **Barnes & Noble** are the most popular chain stores for new books, but there are many smaller local shops and local chains that shouldn't be overlooked, such as **Barbara's Bookstore.** The neighborhoods around Chicago's two most famous universities are goldmines for the book lover, whether shopping for new or used books. Hyde Park and Evanston are the places to go for these.

Computers: CompUSA (1-800-COMPUSA) and **Computer City** (1-800-THE-CITY) have an expanding number of Chicagoland locations. Call their 800 numbers to find the one nearest you. A good downtown store is **Elek-Tek** at 175 W. Jackson.

Discount Department Stores: The national chains with Chicago-land outlets are **K-Mart**, **Target**, **Wal-Mart**, and **Venture**. Suburban locations are ubiquitous, city locations relatively rare.

Electronic Equipment: Televisions, telephones, VCRs, and stereo equipment are sold by department stores, discount stores, and appliance superstores such as **Best Buy** and **Audio Consultants.**

Furniture: There are numerous chain and independent stores everywhere in the city and all have some arrangement for delivery. Prices vary considerably for this service as well as for the furniture so it pays to shop around quite a lot. Among the chains at the low end is **Jennifer**; you'll see their ads on the CTA. Middle market is **Pier One Imports** and **Homemakers**. More pricey and trendy is **Crate & Barrel.**

Hardware: **Ace** and **True Value** are the local chains, with numerous locations all over Chicagoland.

Jewelry: Along with most other things that you can spend a fortune on, North Michigan Avenue is the place to go. Also check out the **Jewelers Center** downtown, 5 South Wabash: 165 jewelers on 13 floors, both wholesale and retail.

Music and Musical Instruments: To do everything in one place, try the **Music Mart** at 333 South State Street. The **Jazz Record Mart** claims to have the world's largest collection of jazz and blues records.

Popular Department Stores: The three most popular stores for a very wide range of consumer goods have numerous branches in suburban shopping malls and fewer in the city. These are **Montgomery Ward, Sears,** and **J.C. Penney.**

Quality Department Stores: The home-grown ones loved by all Chicagoans are **Marshall Field's** and **Carson Pirie Scott.** Both have their main stores in the Loop, and smaller stores located

153

elsewhere in the city and suburbs. Other upscale chain department stores not based in Chicago but with outlets here are **Bloomingdale's** and **Neiman Marcus** (both on Michigan Avenue), and **Nordstrom** (in the Oak Brook Center Mall). **Lord & Taylor** and **Saks Fifth Avenue** (both mostly costly clothing stores) are on Michigan Avenue.

Sporting Goods and Equipment: Sportmart (several Chicagoland locations) is a superstore for everything you need to participate in sports of all kinds, fitness activities, and outdoor pursuits such as hiking and camping.

Mannequins with saris in a window on West Devon Avenue.

The most expensive shopping in Chicago is on and immediately off of **North Michigan Avenue**, also called the **magnificent mile** by those who take such things seriously. Shopping in the Loop is more eclectic, with an equal distribution of quality department stores, specialty shops, and discount outlets of various kinds. Suburban **shopping malls** draw shoppers from a wide area who like to find everything under a single roof in inclement weather. There are few comparable places in the city, though you shouldn't overlook **Chicago Place** and **Water Tower Place** on North Michigan Avenue for high-dollar spending, or **Century Shopping Center** on Clark just north of Diversey for an eclectic mix of shops. The suburban shopping experience nearest the city limits is **Evergreen Plaza Shopping Center** at 97th and Western. Other suburban shopping areas that sometimes draw city shoppers are **Oakbrook Shopping Center** in west suburban Oakbrook, **Northbrook Court Shopping Center** in Northbrook, **Old Orchard Shopping Center** in Skokie, **Woodfield Shopping Center** in west suburban Schaumburg (largest mall in Illinois), and **Gurnee Mills** in north suburban Gurnee, a center for superstores and manufacturers' outlet stores.

Tips about Tipping

We close this chapter with a guide about when it is customary to tip. The general philosophy is that tipping is to show appreciation for good service rendered, or to expedite a service that might otherwise be unacceptably slow. This applies in most situations, but *never* where government employees or police are concerned. Offering money to either of these is seen as an attempted bribe, not a tip, and this is against the law. Which is not to say that it is never done, just that you should never do it. Following is a list of the commonest tipping situations:

- 15 percent in most restaurants, 20 percent in better restaurants, *if the service is good*, and if no service charge has been added to the bill.

155

- A dollar or two, perhaps more, is appreciated by people who deliver food ordered from restaurants to your home; these people are usually poorly paid.
- 15 percent for taxi drivers if they are courteous, professional, and helpful. But if they can't be bothered to get out of the cab and help you with your heavy bags, you shouldn't be bothered either.
- If you check your bags outside with the sidewalk agents at an airport, tip them $1 per bag; no need to tip if you check your bags inside. Skycaps at airports likewise get $1 per bag, more if they perform some extraordinary service.
- Barbers and hairstylists can be tipped 15 percent or more, according to your appreciation of their services.
- Someone who parks your car for you (this is called "valet parking") expects a tip of $2–3, but you needn't tip somebody who simply guides you to a parking place.

CHAPTER EIGHT

YOU AND UNCLE SAM

Gentlemen, get one thing straight once and for all. The policeman isn't there to create disorder; the policeman is there to preserve disorder.
— the late Mayor Richard J. Daley, 1968

In nearly all respects the laws of the United States, the state of Illinois, and local laws apply to people in Chicago equally, whether or not they are U.S. citizens. As a resident of Chicago you are entitled to various privileges and subject to more or less the same legal code as the natives. But you have to play the game by the rules, or you could miss out on what benefits the system has to offer you. This chapter will provide you all the information you need to ensure that your relationship with government authority is on the up and up.

GOVERNMENT MOTIFS

Whether or not American democracy works in practice is a judgment you will have to make for yourself. But the *idea* of democracy is so thoroughly inculcated in the American psyche as to be reflected everywhere, in nearly every institution, so it will benefit you to have some familiarity with its main tenets. It is also worth keeping in mind that if you wish to become an American citizen eventually you will have to demonstrate some familiarity with the system of government, so this is as good a place as any to start.

The central idea about U.S. government is that it is *representative*. People in government, the most important of whom are popularly elected, are seen as servants of the people whose jobs only exist because they must represent the interests of the people who elect them. The system of government enshrined in the U.S. Constitution is taken as a model for government at every level. The various branches of federal government all have their state and local equivalents, though these may go by different names. Government is divided in three branches for administrative purposes, each of which is kept from becoming too powerful by an in-built system of "checks and balances." The branches are the **executive**, represented by an elected leader (the president, state governor, or city mayor, for instance); the **legislative**, consisting of legislative bodies composed of elected representatives (such as the House of Representatives, the Senate, the Illinois Senate, or a city council); and the **judicial**, concerned with enforcement and interpretation of the law and represented by the courts. The judicial branch typically has a larger number of appointed rather than elected officials, but in Illinois many of these officials—judges and top law enforcement officials—are either popularly elected, or their tenure is subject to the approval of voters. From these it can be seen that voters, individual citizens, can have a great deal of influence on politics and government if they are properly organized. In practice a great many people who have the right to vote don't exercise the right: simply because it has always existed for them, they take it for granted, and they may have developed cynical views about the effectiveness of government.

There are two deeply engrained principles of American law that help explain how government works and people's attitude toward it. The first is the U.S. Constitution, a document drafted in 1787 that is the foundation of U.S. law. It includes the Bill of Rights, a set of ten amendments to the original Constitution that guarantee various freedoms of every American citizen. No authority can enact a law that is contrary to the U.S. Constitution; such a law would eventually be declared **unconstitutional**, and would be thrown out by the courts. Thus Americans are guaranteed the protection of the law in many very important areas of life. Whatever complaining Americans may do about their government, most of them are fiercely patriotic about its foundations, and most of them regard the Bill of Rights as a kind of sacred text.

The second principle is itself one of the articles of the Bill of Rights and is usually referred to informally as "states' rights." It says that any area of legislation not specifically mentioned in the Constitution as being the business of the federal government is *not* the business of the federal government, and so is left to individual states, or to the people, to decide. One purpose of this article is to avoid "big government" and to avoid the very real danger of the government taking too much power and interfering in areas of public and private life in which it has no business. The article also recognizes the principle that people have the right to self-determination (individualism rearing its head again) and should not be subject to rules conceived and implemented from afar. This principle is evident in Americans' innate distrust of government regulation and the attitude that the government, at any level, has a case to prove for any legislation that it puts forth, especially legislation that in some way limits people's freedom.

The phenomenon of states' rights is also responsible for the wide variety of laws that exist in the United States, and the fact

159

that what may be perfectly legal in one state may be illegal, or not even legislated about, in another. Despite the possibility of wide disparities, there is in fact quite a lot of uniformity in laws from state to state within regions. The Midwest, of which Illinois is an integral part, tends to be a "middle-of-the-road" area of the country. It is not as conservative as many states in the South, but not as liberal as states in the Northeast or on the West Coast. The state as a whole has voted Republican in more presidential elections than not, and indeed it was Illinois that gave the nation its first Republican president: Abraham Lincoln. But the city of Chicago has always voted staunchly Democrat. All of the five counties surrounding Chicago, and especially Du Page county, are deeply Republican, but Cook County, dominated by Chicago, is firmly in the hands of the Democratic Party.

Local government in the United States is very local indeed, with the boundaries of jurisdiction not extending beyond the city limits. This means that in Chicagoland there are hundreds of local governments, all with rules and regulations peculiar to life within their boundaries. It would be impractical to go into detail about them all, so we present here a short summary of what local governments are responsible for and what they might expect of you. Details of the structure of local government is provided for the City of Chicago and for Cook County only, but if you live in the suburbs or outside of Cook County, you can safely assume that analogous systems are in place.

The City of Chicago

The city is divided politically into 50 wards, and these are in turn divided into precincts. Each ward is represented by an alderman (who may be female, though the terms alderperson or alderwoman have not gained much currency). The 50 aldermen make up the City Council, which together with the mayor, runs Chicago. The mayor is elected by direct popular vote, like all of the aldermen within their wards, which means that it is entirely possible, though in practice not usual, for the mayor to be in conflict with the council. Both mayor and aldermen are elected for terms of four years. In the most recent election, held in February 1999, Mayor Richard M. Daley won reelection to his third full term by a landslide, garnering 73 percent of the vote. He called the victory "a vote of confidence in our city."

Whether you take an interest in local politics or not, it is a good idea to know at least who your alderman is if you live in the

A Chicago policeman on crowd duty in the Loop.

161

city of Chicago; a call to the alderman's office is often the best way to get the attention of any department of city government, rather than trying to deal with the bureaucracy itself. You can find out who your alderman is by consulting your neighbors, and you can find the alderman's phone number under his name in the white pages of the telephone directory. Alternatively, if you learn the number of your ward, there is a spotty alphabetical listing of ward offices by number in the white pages.

Cook County

The main legislative body of Cook County (which includes Chicago and several adjacent suburbs) is the Cook County Board of Commissioners, who are popularly elected by each of the single 17 districts that constitute Cook County. Various other county officials are popularly elected, including the state's attorney (public prosecutor), the superintendent of schools, and the county clerk. Needless to say, voters living in the city of Chicago have a large say in the running of the county, being so numerous in relation to the county population as a whole. The county is responsible for maintaining some roads, jails, and recreational spaces (such as forest preserves). It assesses real estate taxes, which are used largely to fund education.

THE STATUS OF IMMIGRANTS

America is a nation of immigrants and Chicago is a city of immigrants, but not all immigrants are treated equal. For a start, it depends on how long you've been here and what the basis of your residency is. Chances are if you are in, bound for, or even contemplating life in the United States you have already educated yourself about the options available to you concerning residency so we will provide only a rough overview here, with some ideas about where you can learn more.

If you are not an American citizen by birth or married to one, there is no automatic or easy way to gain entry to the United

States. But America is an easier nut to crack than many countries and still takes in large numbers (nearly one million) of immigrants every year. There are four main categories by which foreigners may legitimately gain entry as U.S. residents:

- **Work:** If a U.S. employer can demonstrate a good reason for hiring you—as opposed to some out-of-work American—to do a job, the channels for securing provisional residency (a "green card") are fairly straightforward. The employer completes forms that are submitted to the Department of Labor. If this department is satisfied that you are properly qualified and won't be taking work away from an American, it issues a labor certificate. With this in hand you can apply for a green card with form I-140, *Immigrant's petition for alien worker.* Less than 10 percent of foreigners living in the Chicago area come in under a work-related arrangement.

- **Study:** To be admitted as a full-time student to live in the United States, you must first be admitted by an institution of higher learning via their normal application process. This means in almost all cases that you must pass the TOEFL exam (to demonstrate proficiency in English) as well as meet the requirements for admission of the particular school. In principle, your right to residency in the United States ends when your status as a full-time student ends. In practice, foreign students who go on to make the United States their home after completing their studies are legion. It is usually not difficult to finagle a way to do this; securing work, studying for longer than five years, or getting an American spouse are the time-honored methods.

- **Joining a Family Member:** This category accounts for the largest number of immigrants in Chicagoland, two-thirds of the total. In the majority of cases, a new immigrant is sponsored by a previous immigrant who is an immediate family member (parent, child, or sibling) and who has now become an American citizen. If you are a green card holder you can sponsor your husband, wife, or unmarried children. If you are a U.S. citizen over the age of 21 you can sponsor your husband, wife, any children, your parents, your brothers, and your sisters. All of this is done with form I-130.

- **Asylum:** The United States is a signatory of the 1951 U.N. Convention and Protocol relating to the Status of Refugees, like most developed nations, and thus entertains applications for asylum from persecuted people. Refugees and asylum seekers constitute about 14 percent of foreigners in Chicagoland.

The Crap Shoot

A smaller but widely publicized and largely misunderstood means of entering the United States as a legal foreign resident is the "lottery" conducted each year to attract applicants from parts of the world that normally supply a disproportionately small number of immigrants. It is sometimes called the "diversity visa lottery," or DV lottery for short. The essence of this program is well summed up by the word "lottery," which suggests something to which many are called but few are chosen. In the most recent year reported, 50,000 visas were issued for the 6 million applications submitted, making your chances of success less than one in a hundred. But this is still quite a lot better than most other lotteries you might enter. The stakes are low, and the jackpot is huge if a home in America is what you have always craved.

The lottery is only open to people from countries that do not already have a large number of U.S. visa applicants. If you are from Canada, China, Colombia, the Dominican Republic, El Salvador, Haiti, India, Jamaica, Mexico, the Philippines, Poland, South Korea, Vietnam, or Britain, you are *not* eligible for the lottery. If you enter it anyway, your application will be rejected and any money you spent to have it prepared will be wasted. If you are from some other country, seek advice from your U.S. embassy or consulate. An industry exists to service the hopes of those who want to enhance their chances in the lottery, and many practitioners in this industry are frauds, so you should investigate very carefully anybody who says they can help you in this process. Don't hesitate to ask very specific questions about the process, and don't be satisfied with vague answers.

A Foot in the Door?

Another method of gaining very insecure entry to the United States that cannot be recommended at all is to overstay a conventional visitor's visa. While it is illegal, and foreigners who attempt to gain entry by this method are subject to immediate deportation, thousands of the 500 million visitors to the United States each year overstay their visits, most of them in order to work. The INS (U.S. Immigration and Naturalization Service) spends a disproportionate amount of its enforcement budget on trying to stop the millions of would-be immigrants who attempt to cross the Mexican border every year, but it has announced plans to track down a greater number of other illegal overstayers. There is nothing to recommend this method of "back door" immigration, but it is a perennial favorite because up to now there has been very little likelihood of being caught, especially for Europeans or English-speaking people from other parts of the world who would not by their nature arouse the suspicion of authorities.

Immigration Information

The INS, which is a part of the Justice Department, maintains a site on the World Wide Web that has up-to-date information and downloadable forms pertaining to most matters of work, immigration, and naturalization in the United States. Their homepage is located at **www.ins.usdoj.gov.** By patient navigating you can find on this site nearly everything you would want to know, and probably many things you don't, about immigration into the United States. If you want to go in at the deep end you can even download the nearly 500-page Immigration and Nationality Act to

165

The line forms on the left at the Immigration and Naturalization Service in the Loop.

investigate the labyrinthine ins and outs of living in the United States. This is the most reliable source of information you will find about immigration. A lot of general questions you may have about immigration and naturalization can be answered by listening to prerecorded telephone messages prepared by the INS. Within the United States you can call (800) 375-5283 to listen to these recordings in English or Spanish. You can also order forms over the telephone if you know which forms you need by calling (800) 870-3676.

There is a glut of other unofficial information available to the aspiring U.S. resident on the World Wide Web. Most of it is sponsored by law firms, whose intention is to convince you that if you attempt the application process without their help, you are bound to fail. This presents a dilemma for the would-be U.S. resident, who must either immerse himself in the not very user-friendly official information available (on the web or from U.S. embassies and consulates), or fork over money to an immigration lawyer or advocate. The method you choose in the end probably depends on your means and the amount of time and energy you have to put into the project. One of the most comprehensive private sites on the web for immigration is **www.us-immigration.com**, which takes you to the American Immigration Center. Note that this is a commercial enterprise and has no official status. The site answers a lot of questions, but almost always in a way that plants the lingering suspicion that somebody wants your money!

Visa Information

Visas to visit the United States, whether for business or for pleasure, are handled by a different government department: the Department of State. You can contact a representative of this department at the U.S. embassy or consulate in the country where you live, or you can visit the State Department's website at **www.state.gov**. Searching for information about visas on this site will answer any questions you may have. Residents of 26 countries (as of 1999) who wish to visit the United States for 90 days or less are not required to obtain visas to visit the United States; they need only fill in a form before arriving, which is supplied by international carriers. Countries in the Visa Waiver program include all of the European Union (except Greece and Portugal); the European principalities of Andorra, Liechtenstein, and Monaco; Norway, Switzerland, English-speaking Australasia, Brunei, Iceland, Japan, and Slovenia. This list is subject to change at any time.

Naturalization

If you have been living in the United States for at least five years legally and are at least 18 years old (or three years legally married to a U.S. citizen or legal resident) you can apply for U.S. citizenship, or naturalization. This carries many benefits, among them the right to vote, the right to sponsor other family members to join you in the United States, and the freedom to travel on a U.S. passport. In order to qualify for citizenship, you must be able to read and write simple English (there are some exceptions for elderly people), and you must master basic facts about the history and form of government in the United States. You apply for naturalization with a form N-400. It takes about eight months to schedule an interview from the time you apply.

SOCIAL SECURITY AND TAXES

Whether you are a citizen or not, your presence as a wage earner in the United States (or a dependent of one) requires you to participate in two programs that affect all Americans: Social Security and income tax. Social Security funds old-age pensions, disability pensions, and various other benefits for nonworking Americans and is itself funded by contributions from employers and people who work. Income taxes are separate and go to fund the workings of government. Anyone who earns money is required to pay taxes to both the federal and state governments.

The Social Security System

If you are going to work in Chicago for wages or if you are going to earn money in some other way in Chicago you are required to participate in the Social Security system. This is for your own good. Even if you don't ultimately retire in the United States, chances are that contributions that you pay into the Social Security system can be paid to you in whatever part of the world you choose to spend your twilight years. If you have paid into an equivalent system in some other part of the world, chances are pretty good that the United States, through reciprocal agreements, can have your U.S. contributions credited to your retirement income in the country of your choice.

The cornerstone of the Social Security system is the Social Security number. It is called SSN or simply "social," for short. Your SSN is a number in the format 000-00-0000 that uniquely identifies you among all American taxpayers and is also used by a number of other authorities and organizations. You should make it one of your earliest priorities to get a Social Security card, on which will be printed your name and unique number. Every employer you have will require a Social Security number, and you will also need it to get a driver's license, a credit card, and to open a bank account. You can get an application for a Social Security card at any Social Security office. There are numerous offices in Chicagoland, many of which offer services in foreign languages (Spanish, Polish, Cantonese, and Mandarin); see the listing in the U.S. Government section of the telephone directory (white pages). Alternatively, you can download the application form (SS-5) from the Social Security Administration's website, **www.ssa.gov/online/ss-5.pdf**. Note that you must have proof of legal residency in the United States before you can apply for a Social Security number.

While many institutions require your Social Security number for their records, you should not give it out when you don't have to. Banks, credit card companies, employers, government agencies, and stores that you may want to open a credit account with are entitled to know your number. There is rarely a need to give it to anybody else, and if you are asked for it, you should inquire why it is needed. It is necessary to guard the privacy of your number to some degree because in principle, anyone who has it can gain access to your credit history and possibly to other confidential information about you.

You and the Taxman

If you reside in the United States and you have an income you are liable for federal income tax; it's as simple as that. The complications come later, when you start trying to figure out how much you have to pay, or how much you can avoid paying. You would be hard pressed to find another country in the world where the consumer is deluged with so much detailed information concerning taxes as Americans are. Many simply throw up their hands and turn the whole business of figuring taxes over to an accountant or a tax preparation service. Read on to decide if this is the approach that you want to take.

The income tax system is administered by a federal agency called the Internal Revenue Service, or the IRS for short. Every earning or income-collecting American or U.S. resident is required to file a tax return with the IRS every April 15, which covers the previous calendar year's income. If you are married, you and your spouse can file a joint return. At the end of your first taxable year in the United States, which for practical purposes will be the first December 31st that you spend as a resident, you should start thinking about your tax return and collecting the various documents that you will need to figure your taxes. Most of these will be sent to you automatically, by your employer, contractors, banks, savings institutions, and brokers, depending on the source of your income.

You will not receive a tax return form and instructions in the mail the first year you are required to file because the IRS, in principle, doesn't know about you yet. You will have to collect forms where they are distributed to the public: in post offices, banks, some libraries, in the Federal Building in downtown Chicago, and over the Internet at **www.irs.gov**. At the very least you will need the booklet, running to some 100 pages, that contains

form 1040 (the standard income tax return) as well as copies of most of the commonest supporting forms. As a foreigner in the United States your tax situation is probably not as straightforward as that of the ordinary American, especially if you have some income from abroad. For that reason, you should either seek expert tax help from an accountant or count on spending a fair amount of time poring over publications of the IRS to try to figure out things for yourself. The average tax preparation service (H&R Block is the best-known one) is used to dealing with Americans with more typical situations. You shouldn't assume that they will know all the ins and outs of your tax situation. If you need outside help, it is better for you to seek advice from your compatriots or from your consulate.

People with very high incomes normally engage the services of an accountant to find tax shelters and loopholes that will enable them to reduce their taxes. For the ordinary person, more modest options are available. Three simple ways of reducing your federal income tax are 1) open an individual retirement account (IRA), contributions to which are tax-deductible; 2) donate money to recognized charities, as these contributions are also largely tax-deductible; and 3) buy a home in Chicagoland—interest you pay on the mortgage is tax-deductible and amounts to a hefty sum over the course of a year.

Other Taxes You Have to Pay

In addition to your federal income tax, you are liable for state income tax as well. Most state governments circulate tax forms similar to and based on the federal ones. You always calculate your federal income tax first, and then use those figures to fill out your state form. As with the federal forms, you will not receive these automatically the first year you are resident in Chicagoland. It is your responsibility to acquire the forms (from a bank, post office, public library, or the downtown Thompson Center, which is a state office building) and file them yourself. All three states in

171

the Chicagoland area (Illinois, Wisconsin, Indiana) require residents to pay state income tax, but all have different ways of calculating it. In Illinois and Indiana the income tax rate is about 3 percent, in Wisconsin it is about 6 percent.

There are a number of other taxes collected by governments, but these are normally paid at the point of sale, either added onto or included in the price of what you buy.

Façades old and new juxtaposed in the Loop: City Hall and the Thompson Center (State of Illinois building).

CHAPTER NINE

CHICAGO AT WORK
AND IN SCHOOL

It is a remarkable thing to meet such an assemblage of educated, refined, and wealthy persons as may be found there, living in small, inconvenient houses on the edge of the wind prairie.

— Harriet Martineau (visiting in 1840)

Unless your coming to Chicago results from marriage or following up family connections, chances are that your tenure in the Windy City is because of work or study. We have left a discussion about these two important activities until rather late since they come largely with a built-in structure that initially requires you only to do what everyone else is doing, rather than figure out everything on your own from the outset. Our focus in this chapter

173

then, beyond a brief overview of the worlds of work and studying in Chicago, is a short guide to the unwritten rules that govern both activities. These may help you to decipher what might otherwise be incomprehensible behavior among your new Midwestern peers.

THE CITY WORKPLACE

In work as in most other spheres of life, Americans show a penchant for comfort and informality, and Chicagoans are no exception. There are professions where everyone wears business suits, especially in law and the financial world, but even here a custom of "dress-down Friday" has made some inroads and the crisp uniform is slightly relaxed on the last workday of the week. Women in jobs that require professional dress often wait until they are in the office to put on the most burdensome part of the uniform, that is, the shoes, and so women on the street are often seen, incongruously, dressed in expensive suits along with white socks and running shoes.

In interpersonal relations at work, American informality expresses itself in the lack of obvious signs of rank within the workplace. Nearly everyone addresses everyone else by a given name or a nickname. Titles such as Mr. and Mrs. are rarely used in direct address by people who deal with each other every day. Your colleagues will either be introduced to you or will introduce themselves by the name they wish to be called, and you can use it thereafter. The only common exception to this practice is in medical settings, where doctors are usually addressed by "Dr.," followed by a surname. For dealing with people you don't know and who won't be introduced because of circumstances, "Sir" is a useful courtesy title for a man, especially if he is older than you. "Ma'am" is acceptable to most women, especially those older than you; "Miss" is usually acceptable to younger women. Some other people encountered casually can be addressed by their work titles: "Officer" for a police officer, "Driver" for a bus or taxi driver, "Waiter" (as long as it is not shouted) for a waiter.

The emphasis on ease should not give the impression that Chicagoans are lax in their approach to work. The so-called "Protestant ethic"—the notion that hard work is virtuous and will be rewarded with good fortune—is as strong in Chicago as anywhere in the land. People in salaried professions (those not paid at an hourly rate) all have official starting and stopping times at work but may take scant notice of them, particularly at the end of the day. In certain offices the prevailing rule is simply to stay at work until the work is done, which means in effect that many professionals put in much more than the standard 35–40 hour work week.

Division of Labor

The customs in Chicagoland regarding salaried vs. hourly workers, and union vs. nonunion labor, are similar to what is found in most parts of the developed world, and similar to the pattern that prevails in most American cities. Traditionally the United States has been more highly unionized in the older eastern and northern industrial cities than in the western and southern cities. Workers in cities in general tend to be more organized than workers outside of cities. The pattern of unionization in Chicago follows that of most northern industrial cities, that is, highly unionized in some trades. Though there are many exceptions, a rule of thumb is that workers who do not require a university degree but whose work involves some formal training or an apprenticeship are unionized; such workers are typically paid hourly. Workers with a university degree are more typically salaried, and not unionized.

The majority of Chicagoland hourly-paid workers in skilled trades enjoy a comfortable standard of living, and as a result they are not inclined as a group to be militant or uncooperative, whether members of a union or not. This is the pattern that prevails generally in the United States. Disputes between labor and management tend to be small and scattered and do not usually last long.

175

Occasionally strikes affect a national company or industry, typically airlines or car manufacturing, and these disputes are highly publicized but usually quickly resolved. It is rare for government at any level to intervene in disputes between unions and management. The notion of a general strike or widespread labor disruption is unheard of today in the United States.

Doing as the Natives Do

In the past quarter of a century a great deal of attention has been brought to bear on the ethnic and cultural diversity of American cities. Many government programs have been introduced at different times to ensure that ethnic and cultural minorities are given the same opportunities that the so-called "white majority" enjoys. While there is still a great deal of disparity in many areas of life, particularly in housing and economic opportunity, the result of affirmative action and other programs aimed at promoting minorities is that at least the appearance of equality has been achieved in the workplace, and people of all ethnic and racial backgrounds work together in the same place.

The effect of this diversity in the workplace is that many people are already used to working in a multicultural environment. You, as an arriving foreigner, are therefore fairly unlikely to be the first foreigner in your workplace, and perhaps even unlikely to be the first person of your nationality in your workplace, unless your origins are remote or exotic. Working Chicagoans, particularly those in large companies or whose work requires a university degree, are moderately inured to rubbing shoulders with people of different nationalities. When you combine this fact with the indelible American cultural value of individuality, what emerges is the news that you don't really have to be concerned, in broad terms, about whether you will "fit in." Of course you will fit in, because everyone does. All that is expected of you is that you be yourself.

The Merchandise Mart, a sea of offices docked on the Chicago River.

With that much said, it must be noted that there are marked veins of conformity in most areas of American life. For all the emphasis placed on individual freedom and diversity, Americans are in many ways more conformist than their European counterparts in small things. Midwesterners, being more conservative culturally than their coastal counterparts, are more conformist still. The mainstream of conduct and decorum is fairly narrow in these small matters. It is a good idea to have a handle on which of them applies in the workplace, so that you don't end up distinguishing yourself in a way that causes you (and others) discomfort. Behavior in the following matters is more or less standard among Chicagoans in the workplace, and deviation from the standard won't benefit you in any way:

Body Contact: There is a wide spectrum of permissible types and styles of body contact among Americans, because of individual

177

temperaments and different cultural backgrounds. In the professional atmosphere that prevails in most workplaces, there is almost no touching or physical contact between people of the opposite sex; it would be viewed as inappropriate and suggestive. Many people, however, use physical contact as part of their communication style, so you should not be alarmed by a friendly hand on the shoulder, arm, or back from a colleague of the same sex. If it is something natural for you to do, you need not hesitate to use such gestures yourself on colleagues of the same sex. Body contact between women is usually more frequent and informal than between men. Handshakes, whether between people of the same or opposite sexes, are brief, lasting no more than a couple of seconds.

Directness: In all your dealings with people at work, direct expression is always the safest course. Many cultures of the world have elaborate, indirect, and subtle forms of communication that are designed to make sure that nobody loses face or experiences shame or humiliation. American culture is not one of these. When you mean no, say no. If you don't understand something, ask for clarification. When you want something, ask for it directly; don't spend any time devising an elaborate context, the aim of which is to deliver a subtle message to somebody that you work with. The message will probably be lost and you will have wasted your time. If you have a message to get across, just formulate the words and say them. This will be a new and not always comfortable way of dealing with people if you come from a culture where communication is more subtle, but it is worthwhile making the effort to learn directness. It is what Americans understand best.

Egalitarianism: Never forget that Americans are instilled with the idea of democracy and majority rule from the time that they are toddlers. By the time they are working adults, this results in the idea that everybody's opinion is of value, but nobody's is sacrosanct. It is not unusual for Americans to question authority, and it is common for all people in a workplace, regardless of their professional status, to be consulted on matters that affect people equally. Americans are much more comfortable with decisions arrived at by consensus than with ones handed down from on high. If your opinion is solicited on a matter at work, don't hesitate to share it. If you do not voice your opinion or if you never seem to have one, you may be viewed as a "pushover," somebody whom it is easy to take advantage of.

Elevators: Elevators, or lifts as you may think of them, are the locus of highly ritualized behavior that can be unnerving if you haven't experienced it before. The principle at work is that everyone is entitled to his or her own personal space. Since this is impossible in the confines of an elevator, everyone settles for the next best thing, which is to create a sort of social vacuum around him- or herself. After you enter the elevator you turn around and face the front, having pushed the button corresponding to the floor where you will get out. If it is too crowded for you to reach the button panel, it is reasonable to say, for example, "twenty-seven, please" to someone standing near the panel. Thereafter you stand rigidly as if under military inspection, moving only to leave or let someone behind you leave. If you are traveling in an elevator with a companion it is suitable to stand together, but don't carry on a loud conversation that will disturb others. This rigid protocol is relaxed to some degree in apartment buildings where you are likely to know or be known to fellow passengers.

Punctuality: You should try to do everything *on time* with regard to your work, and that means at the time announced or requested. It is better to be a couple of minutes early for appointments and meetings than five minutes late. You should also expect that when you name a time for somebody to meet you, that is the time they will honor. And they do expect you to name a particular time, not

179

to be vague. It is usually specific enough to name a time on the hour, half hour, or quarter hour, but don't be surprised if people are even more specific. The same punctuality should be respected with regard to deadlines. If you are told something is to be finished by a particular time, *that* is the time it should be finished.

Relations Between the Sexes: In the workplace, men and women in the same job enjoy the same status. To put it another way, status in the workplace is not based on sex in any way, but on the job. If you are a man, whatever your cultural background, you must treat women in your workplace as equals in every way. Women, similarly, can expect equal treatment from men. Men should be careful not to let sexual innuendo be a part of their dealings with women in the workplace. Litigation involving sexual harassment is a growth industry at the present time. A remark that you consider innocent and even complimentary could be construed as degrading to a woman if it is thought to put her in a subservient role or to regard her as an object. If you have any confusion about this you should discuss it with American colleagues, but the safest course is to treat people of the opposite sex with the same courtesy and respect that you use with people of your own sex.

Smoking: Smoking is not allowed in office buildings and people who smoke are increasingly viewed as social pariahs, except by each other, of course. You will see "smokers' huddles" on the street outside office buildings where smokers gather even in the most inclement weather to feed their habit. If you are a smoker and have given some thought to quitting, there is no better time than now, before you settle in Chicago.

Business and Politics
The business culture of Chicago does not differ very much from that in other cities, except insofar as it is animated mostly by Midwesterners. For that reason it is a little more straightforward,

practical, and down-to-earth than you might find on either of the coasts. A possible shortcoming of the practical viewpoint is that it neglects the long view. People in business are very often geared to meeting deadlines, producing results, and making apparent progress. All efforts are directed toward these goals, sometimes without adequate consideration of their long-term effects.

All levels of government—local, state, and federal—have traditionally followed a *laissez-faire* attitude toward business. The philosophy is that if you let the free market take care of itself, it will serve its purpose and work most effectively. For this reason there is mistrust of any government intervention in business. The Republican Party is the greatest proponent of "hands-off" government (in theory, anyway) and so is associated with big business. The Democratic Party, today almost imperceptibly to the left of the Republicans, has been associated historically with big-spending government programs, alliance with labor unions, and attempts to regulate business and the economy.

While it is rare for government to directly intervene in the affairs of the business world—in a labor dispute, for example—unless of course laws are being broken, it is quite common for the business world to intervene in the affairs of government. This does not happen in any official way, but in a way sanctioned by long practice. The business community largely funds the election campaigns of elected officials. In addition the huge lobbying industry—whereby businesses and trade organizations hire professionals to persuade and cajole legislators to take stands on issues that favor business—ensures that no legislation will be passed that is completely inimical to the interests of big business.

In recent years the relationship between government and business has resulted in a tension felt by all Americans. It is common to perceive a conflict between "corporate America"—a term for large corporations collectively that are believed to really run the United States—and the individual or family, who is seen to be

Loop workers wait for a river bridge to be lowered on West Madison Street.

at the mercy of the faceless, impersonal, profit-driven economic giants. Many Americans today feel that their elected officials are in fact owned by the business community, and that big business, not the will of the people, is what really sets the agenda in Washington, in Springfield, or in the workings of city government.

The term "corporate welfare," very much in currency today, refers to the fact that the only purpose of many laws is to cushion big businesses—to provide it tax incentives, government handouts, and leniency in all matters of regulation—so that businesses can pursue profits without any check on their voraciousness. Resentment arises because it is the ordinary taxpayer, through payment of income tax, who funds this arrangement. Some people also think it unfair that while there is a very active program under way to cut ordinary welfare—the programs that aid the poorest people in society—there is very little evidence that legislators are interested in cutting corporate welfare. The popular inference is that legislators do not dare to challenge big business, because they would not be able to win reelection if they did.

This negative perception of big business does not mean that people who work in the business world are the subject of resentment. The angry feelings are mostly directed against people and entities who do not present a human face: boards of directors and the very top executives of very large and successful corporations, especially multinational corporations.

Self-Employment

If you have the proper credentials for residency in Chicago, discussed in the previous chapter, you may wish to forego the entire regimented employment scene and start your own business. You can go into business in a number of different ways. If your goal is self-employment, there are not many complications other than paying your taxes. Self-employed people pay the same tax as everyone else, plus self-employment tax. This is the equivalent of the Social Security contributions that employees and their employers pay, and covers the cost of unemployment benefits and old-age pensions. Numerous guides are available to steer the self-employed person in the right direction in this regard; these are available in any good bookstore.

If you have loftier goals, for instance doing business as a corporation, partnership, or limited liability company, you should seek the advice of a lawyer and an accountant, although for the truly pioneering in spirit there are do-it-yourself guides available for this too, available in bookstores. You should buy a guide about incorporating a business in the state of Illinois, since laws governing corporations vary from state to state. If you obtained your residency in the United States in connection with your employment, that employment is a condition of your residency and you cannot elect to become self-employed without formality.

Alien Entrepreneurship

There is a category of immigration that may be available to those wishing to reside in the United States but not meeting any of the standard qualifications for doing so. The basic requirement is lots of money and commercial know-how. If you can prove to the satisfaction of authorities that you can start a business in the United States capitalized to the tune of about $1,000,000 that will employ at least ten U.S. citizens or legal aliens, you may be able to gain entry on that basis alone. For details (which are many and complicated) you should consult an immigration lawyer or read the pertinent sections of the Immigration and Nationality Act (see the previous chapter).

EDUCATION IN CHICAGO

Education is the full-time pursuit of three-quarters of a million Chicagoans, from primary school to graduate school. In addition to the half-million schoolchildren in grades K-12 (explanation below), there are about 250,000 students in higher education, in Chicagoland's many state and private colleges and universities. This brief survey of education in Chicago will give you the information you need to arrange the best education for your children or for yourself. We start at entry level, with an overview of the system of compulsory education for children.

K-12 Education

Although primary and secondary education in the United States is under the control of state governments, with considerable autonomy granted to individual school districts, it is remarkably uniform throughout the country. So if your children have already attended American schools, either in the United States or abroad, their integration into the system in Chicago will be seamless. If the American education system is new to you, here are a few basic facts with pertinent terminology highlighted:

- Compulsory and free education is for all children from age 6, but in practice children usually begin their formal education with **kindergarten** at age 5. Kindergartners attend school for usually half a day, either in the morning or afternoon, otherwise following the same schedule of holidays and breaks as older children.

- Compulsory education ends at grade 12, when students graduate with a **high school diploma** at about age 17. (This is the source of the term "**K-12 education**," meaning education for children in kindergarten through the 12th grade.) A high school diploma is the minimum requirement for entry into higher education, further vocational education, and jobs of just about any kind except the most unskilled variety. Young people who "drop out" of school without getting a high school diploma are generally regarded as failures who will eventually turn to crime or drugs if they haven't done so already. There are very few jobs anywhere for **high school dropouts**.

- Schoolchildren in grades 1 through 6 normally attend what is called a **grade school; primary school** and **elementary school** mean the same thing. Students in grades 7 and 8, sometimes grade 9, attend a **junior high school**, also called a **middle school**. Grades 9 to 12 (sometimes only 10 to 12) are in a **high school**. Students in 9th grade are called **freshmen**; 10th graders are **sophomores**; 11th graders are **juniors**, 12th graders are **seniors**.

- The school year starts in late August or early September (exact dates differ from one school district to another) and runs until late May or early June. There are holidays of about two weeks over the period that includes Christmas and New Year, and one or two weeks in the spring, normally around the spring equinox, which sometimes includes Easter. In addition schoolchildren have all state and federal holidays off. The school day usually begins around 8:30 in the morning and is normally finished by 3:30 in the afternoon. Students attend school Monday through Friday.

- Children's school work is assessed continuously, usually by using a grading system with letters A to D and F. **A** is for exceptional or outstanding work, **B** is for satisfactory work, **C** is for average work, **D** is for unsatisfactory work, and **F** is for failing work. These letters can be further modified with a + or –, e.g. B+, C–. Several times during the school term schoolchildren are given "**report cards**," showing their grades in all subjects. The report card should be a fair assessment of your child's progress in school. You should always take a look at it. Some schools require you to sign it.

- Children may have the opportunity to participate in some of their school's **extra-curricular activities**. Most schools have sports teams that compete in league play with teams from other schools of similar size. Other activities may include drama clubs, marching bands, debating societies, and the like.

Children board a school bus at a public elementary school.

Which School?

Several factors determine which of Chicago's more than 500 schools your child will attend. All of Chicago and its suburbs are divided into school districts, with each district educating all the children within its borders. If you make no further arrangements for your children, they will be expected to attend the designated school for the area in which you live. There are, however, several other arrangements you can make for your child, and it is in your child's best interest for you to educate yourself about the system and so make the most intelligent choice of school. Many of the Chicago suburbs have public schools with excellent reputations and very good educational programs. Public schools in the city of Chicago, especially those in poor neighborhoods (except for some of the special schools mentioned below) can be riddled with every variety of problem (administrative disputes, drugs, violence, and the like). So before you blithely enroll your child in the local school, consider some of the other options. In addition to the regular public schools, Chicagoland also offers:

- **Parochial Schools:** There are a large number of schools in Chicagoland with religious affiliation. The leader in the field is the Roman Catholic Church, with 180 schools in Chicago alone, of which 30 are high schools, educating more than 75,000 children. There are also a large number of Lutheran schools, and a smaller but significant number of Jewish schools. Parochial schools generally have a much better rate of academic success than public schools (that is, more of their graduates go on to higher education), and they take, in general, a more traditional approach to education than their public counterparts. A modern outgrowth of the parochial school is the so-called Christian school, one affiliated with an evangelical sect that teaches creationism and the like instead of traditional science.

- **Magnet Schools:** These are part of the public school system, but they accept students by application only. The magnet

187

elementary schools (36 in number) try to achieve a multicultural balance by drawing children proportionally from all of Chicago's rich diversity of communities. The nine magnet high schools each offer concentrated specialization in various areas to prepare students for further vocational education, higher education, or work.

- **Other Private Schools:** There are several private Montessori schools that give instruction in languages other than English, and an international school. A comprehensive (if not very indepth) guide to schools in the Chicago area outside the public system is *Chicago School and Daycare Guide* by Andrew Fogaty, published by C.V.S. Press in Chicago. It gives a geographical listing in fixed format of schools and daycare centers all over Chicagoland.

Home Schooling

A movement that is gathering considerable momentum in the United States at present is *home schooling*, in which parents take the responsibility of educating their children at home without sending them to school. The reasons for this are several: a perception that public schools provide inadequate education; the perceived danger or bad influences that children will be exposed to in the school environment, in the form of drugs, gangs, bullies, and the like; and the concern that children will not receive proper spiritual or religious education in public schools. The separation between church and state is enshrined in the U.S. Constitution; public schools are thereby forbidden to engage in religious education. Parents who educate their children at home are typically conservative Christians who wish to inculcate their children in the teachings of the Bible and perhaps to avoid the findings of science that conflict with it.

At present Illinois does not regulate home schooling very rigorously. Individual school districts have the main responsibility for insuring that children not attending regular schools are getting adequate education. It is a huge undertaking to educate children at home if the goal is to prepare them for higher education in the mainstream system, and no parent should embark on home schooling without being fully acquainted with the responsibilities. On the other hand, if you do not think your children will finish their education or take up a career in the United States eventually, you may wish to consider educating them yourself. You should consult your local school district to learn what your responsibilities are. There is also a great deal of support material on the World Wide Web, much of it, though certainly not all, with a strongly Christian flavor.

Higher Education

From high school, children can go on to full-time work, or to further education in a vocational school, a junior college, a community college, or a four-year college (which is more or less the equivalent of university, and in many cases will be a university). Junior colleges and community colleges offer an eclectic range of programs with an emphasis on practical skills and knowledge. The highest degree offered is usually an associate degree, after two years of study. Four-year colleges and universities offer bachelor's degrees (a B.A. or a B.S.), usually after four years of study with a concentration in at least one subject. Finally, universities offer advanced degrees such as master's (M.A. or M.S., at least one year beyond a bachelor's) and doctorates (Ph.D., two to several years after a bachelor's). Universities also offer specialized degrees in their various professional schools, such as MBAs in business schools, JDs in law schools, and various medical qualifications in medical schools.

Chicago's dozen public and more than a dozen private colleges and universities teach some 230,000 students. Three of the country's top research universities are in or near Chicago: the

One of the many gargoyles that festoon the University of Chicago.

University of Chicago in Hyde Park, the University of Illinois at Chicago on the near west side, and Northwestern University in Evanston.

Specific admission requirements at Chicago's institutions of higher education vary widely, but a high school diploma is the minimum. Students who have been educated abroad to the level of the international baccalaureate have probably gone further than the average American high school graduate. Provided such students are fluent in English, they will certainly have met the educational level required for entry into American universities. Any other qualification with which most students in other countries leave secondary education will probably be regarded as at least equivalent to a high school diploma. British A-levels are about the equivalent of first-year undergraduate work in the United States.

Students in secondary education who envision a higher degree normally take the SAT (Scholastic Achievement Test) near the end of high school; colleges use this as a standardized evaluation test for entrants. If your children are being educated abroad but will attend college in the United States, it is important for them to take the SAT. Arrangements for doing so can be made in most developed countries in the world. Contact an American embassy for details.

DAYCARE

We have accounted for everyone's full-time activities in this chapter so far except for preschool children. There are a number of options available to families with two working parents; none of them is cheap, and many would argue that none of them is even desirable. But many parents today turn their children over to the care of others at an early age, and consequently many options are available. To start, you can look in the earlier mentioned *Chicago School and Daycare Guide* by Andrew Fogaty, published by C.V.S. Press in Chicago. There are also listings in the Yellow Pages under "Child Care," "Nanny Service," and under the schools listing, "Nursery Schools," "Kindergartens," and "Academic Pre-Schools."

CHAPTER TEN

CHICAGO AT PLAY

Oh Sodom was some and Gomorra was great—
And in Venice each man's an Iago;
But nothing out there can ever compare
with the sweet state of things in Chicago
 —"Chicago", a popular song of the 19th century

In a published survey of more than 500 American urban communities, Chicago ranks number one in having the best recreational facilities. The parts of the lakefront developed for recreation would alone put Chicago among the top contenders, but you don't have to live near the lake, or even go near it to enjoy some of the many activities and areas devoted to recreation. Read on for an overview of the many ways that you can spend your leisure hours in and around the city, and to learn more about socializing with the natives.

THE GREAT OUTDOORS (AND INDOORS)

The Chicago Park District is the authority in charge of all public outdoor, and many indoor, recreational spaces in the city. Farther afield, individual municipalities operate their own recreational facilities, and Cook County maintains forest preserves at the edge of the metropolitan area. Most of the facilities operated by the Chicago Park District are either free or usable for a very low cost. These include baseball and softball diamonds, basketball backboards, football fields, golf courses, gymnasiums, swimming pools, and tennis courts. In addition, there are more than 500 parks, totaling more than 7,000 acres under the Park District's supervision. If you don't manage to locate facilities near you by any other method, the Chicago Park District telephone listings in the government pages of the telephone directory may be of some help.

The Park District is also in charge of lakefront recreation facilities, including all the running and bicycle trails, swimming beaches, harbors, and harbor facilities. The lake rises above bone-chilling temperatures usually toward the end of June and stays that way, barring the odd day when the water is suddenly cold, throughout August and sometimes into September. The boating season begins in earnest in May and runs, more or less, through the end of October. Fishing is also permitted in the many lagoons and harbors lining the lake front; a fishing license is required. It can be obtained from Park District field houses where there are lagoons, as well as at bait shops or via the Department of Natural Resources. At different times of year, perch, rock bass, salmon, bullheads, catfish, and trout can be hooked.

Standing Attractions

Anyone looking for entertainment and diversion in Chicago is spoiled for choice, as the press entertainment listings will show. That is the best place to look for current programs, times, and

Birds, boats, and buildings: looking south from Diversey Harbor.

schedules of the various entertainment choices. Here is a listing of the most important cultural institutions. They all offer a combination of regular and special programs the year round, or in the case of musical attractions, during certain seasons.

The **Art Institute of Chicago** (Michigan Avenue at Adams) is Chicago's premier showcase for the fine arts and internationally renowned for its collections of Impressionist and American art.

The **Chicago Symphony Orchestra** plays at **Symphony Center** (220 S. Michigan) in the winter and at the **Ravinia Festival** (Highland Park) in the summer.

The Cultural Center (Michigan Avenue between Randolph and Washington) has a few permanent exhibits, such as the **Museum of Broadcast Communications**, but it is mainly a place for temporary exhibitions and performances, and movies. There is nearly always something watchable going on, during the day and in the evening as well. You can pick up a monthly calendar of events at the center. Inside there is a **Chicago Visitor's Center** (at the Randolph Street entrance) where you can pick up brochures about other attractions all over Chicagoland. Admission to all Cultural Center events is free.

The **Lyric Opera** (20 N. Wacker Drive) is Chicago's high-tone, high-dollar opera company, with productions featuring internationally known singers and directors. The main season runs late September through mid-March.

The **Museum Campus** (lakefront from 1200 to 1400 S) is the site of three important attractions: the **Field Museum of Natural History**, which houses everything from the natural world that can be stuffed, reconstructed, mummified, or otherwise made to look nearly lifelike; the **Shedd Aquarium and Oceanarium**, where things from the sea live in nearly natural conditions; and **Adler Planetarium**, where you can see the stars. All three are great places to take kids that afford enjoyment for adults as well.

The **Museum of Science and Industry** (57th Street and Lake Shore Drive) showcases scientific and technical achievements in both historical and contemporary perspectives. It's also a great place to take kids, with lots of hands-on and experimental learning experiences.

Navy Pier (500 N on the lakefront) is primarily an attraction for tourists with restaurants, shops, amusements for children, and docking facilities for cruise and tour boats. It's a great place to take your visitors when they come to see you in Chicago.

Entertaining Children

If you have school-aged children they will probably find their way around the Chicago community more quickly than you will, and they may not want for ideas to amuse themselves. Besides the attractions noted above, children will also enjoy the following:

- Brookfield Zoo in west suburban Brookfield (you can take a train from Union Station or drive) and Lincoln Park Zoo in Lincoln Park
- visits to the observation areas of the tallest downtown buildings (the Sears Tower and the John Hancock Center) on clear days
- boat rides on Lake Michigan and the Chicago River (they leave from Navy Pier and the Michigan Avenue bridge) in pleasant weather

A youngster gets intimate with art, sliding down the Picasso sculpture in Daley Plaza.

Theater and Cinema

Chicago has a thriving theater culture that has been the training ground of many actors and directors who have gone on to achieve national and international acclaim. The *Chicago Reader* has the most complete listing of theater activity, but reviews appear in most other print media as well. Plays and musicals that have proven their durability and appeal on Broadway also come to Chicago; the downtown Schubert Theatre and newly renovated Oriental Theatre are the favorite places for these.

Cinemas (usually called movie theaters) are to be found in every corner of Chicagoland. The current fashion is large new multiplexes that show remarkably little variety in their screenings — perhaps because nearly all of them are owned by the same company! They are the places to see all of Hollywood's latest output; the same film is typically shown at a dozen theaters around the area. A few cinemas have more discriminating taste and are the best choices for revivals of old films, foreign films, and independent films. Nearly all of these are on the North Side. They are the **Biograph**, the **Fine Arts** (downtown), the **Music Box, Piper's Alley**, the **Three-Penny**, and the **Village**.

Real film fans will not want to overlook the annual **Chicago Film Festival**, which takes place every October. Films from around the world are shown at a number of locations. Distinguished directors and well-known stars also make appearances.

Sporting Life

Chicago has a high-profile professional sporting scene and loyal followers to support it. Enthusiasm about professional sports, especially among men, is one of the quickest routes for making American friends. Entire books are devoted to the subtleties of various games. Space does not permit a detailed treatment here, but an explanation of the two purely American games not played extensively abroad, baseball and football, is in order. Here, with important jargon and terminology highlighted, are the basics:

197

Baseball: Two teams of nine players take turns either **batting** (when they can score) or **fielding** (when they try to stop the other team from scoring). One point is awarded for a **run**, which is achieved when a player makes his way all around the **bases** after he has hit a ball. A player whose turn it is to bat is called a **batter;** a player who has hit a ball successfully and is on one of the bases is called a **runner.** If a batter hits the ball out of the ball park or into the spectator stands where no **outfielder** can catch it, he scores a **home run**, making the trip all the way around the bases in one go. When a batter is "up" (taking his turn), he has several chances to hit the ball thrown to him by the **pitcher**. If the pitched ball passes over **home plate** (where the batter stands) between the knees and shoulders of the batter, it is considered a **strike**, whether the batter swings at it or not. If the pitched ball is not within this zone, it is called a **ball**. After four balls, a batter can **walk** to first base just as if he had hit the ball. After three strikes, a batter is **out**. In order to be able to run to first base (or beyond), the batter must hit a **fair ball**, which is a ball that flies forward between the lines radiating out from home plate to first base and third base. If the ball flies outside these lines, it is a **foul ball**. The first two foul balls that a batter hits are considered strikes, but thereafter he may hit an indefinite number with impunity. A batter is also out when a fielder catches his fair ball before it reaches the ground. A runner is out when a fielder gets the ball to the base he is running toward before he gets there. Finally, a runner can be put out by **tagging**, touching him with the ball when he is running between bases. After three players are out, the teams change sides.

The defending team plays nine positions: the pitcher, who throws the balls to the batters and is the most important player; the **catcher**, who crouches behind home plate and catches pitched balls not swung at, when he is not making arcane signals to the pitcher; three **outfielders**, who play far out in the field, ready to catch **fly balls** (balls that are hit a long, high distance); three

basemen, one each at **first base, second base**, and **third base**, which are the points in a diamond shape that the batter must touch as he runs; and finally the **shortstop**, who plays between second base and third base, where many hit balls go. A game consists of nine **innings**, an inning being an instance of each team taking a turn at bat. The first half of the inning is called the **top**, the second half is the **bottom**.

Football: The professional game is divided into four **quarters** of 15 minutes each, during which opposing teams of 11 players each try to score by making touchdowns (see below) after long and arduous attempts to move the ball down the field toward their opponent's goal. The clock is stopped whenever the ball is not in play, so games take generally two hours or more. A long break called **halftime** is provided in the middle of the game.

A game begins by one team **kicking off** to the other, that is, kicking the ball toward them at their end of the field. The team kicked to is the **receiving team.** At this point they take **possession** of the ball and play **offense** (pronounced OFF-ence): that is, they attempt to score by reaching their opponent's goal. The other team plays **defense** (pronounced DEE-fence), that is, they try to keep the offensive team from scoring and get possession of the ball themselves. A **touchdown** (6 points) is scored for the offensive team when they can get the ball across the defending team's goal line, either by a player running with the ball, or a player catching a ball that is passed to him. Fewer points can be scored by two other methods involving kicking the ball, **field goals** and **conversions**.

The ball makes progress by a player running with it (**rushing**), or by a player passing the ball to another player who has run ahead. However, once a player has begun running with the ball, he cannot then pass it ahead. When the player with the ball is successfully stopped by the opposing team, or if the ball goes outside the boundaries of the field, the ball is **dead**. The offensive players then regroup and consider their next **play**. A team in possession is allowed four **downs**, or plays, to move the ball a total of **ten yards** forward. If they are unable to move this distance in four downs, they forfeit possession of the ball. You will notice that the playing field, a large rectangle, is marked off with parallel horizontal lines. These are the yard lines, each separated by ten yards, and called simply the **ten-yard line**, **twenty-yard line**, and so forth. The playing field is 100 yards long (a yard is slightly shorter than a meter). Officials in the game (there are many) can call **fouls** against players or teams for breaking rules. Fouls result in **penalties**, in which the offending team loses yardage, or the offended-against team gets an extra down.

At the beginning of each down, players group along an imaginary line, the **line of scrimmage**; this is the point on the field where play was last stopped. A play begins by a player (the **center**) passing the ball backward between his legs (**snapping** the ball) to the **quarterback**, the key player whose actions mainly decide the course of play. The quarterback can run forward with the ball but more commonly he will pass it off to a nearby player who runs with it (a **running back**), or he passes it forward to a player who has run down the field (a **receiver**). If the quarterback is going to pass the ball, he must do so from behind the line of scrimmage. If he crosses the line of scrimmage with the ball in his hands, his only option is to run with it. While all of this is going on, the defensive team is single-mindedly focused on stopping the player with the ball by throwing him to the ground (**tackling**), or preventing any other player from running forward or receiving a pass (**blocking**). If a player who is carrying the ball or trying to catch the ball drops it, this constitutes a **fumble**, and any player who can get the ball then gets possession of it for his team. It is in general a rough and violent game; players wear helmets and protective padding but nevertheless suffer serious and often long-term injuries.

The following table sets out the Chicago teams that play in national competition, along with other pertinent information.

Team	Sport	Governing Body	Home Field
Chicago Bears	Football	National Football League	Soldier Field
Chicago Black Hawks	Ice Hockey	National Hockey League	United Center
Chicago Bulls	Basketball	National Basketball League	United Center
Chicago Cubs	Baseball	National League	Wrigley Field
Chicago White Sox	Baseball	American League	Comiskey Park
Chicago Wolves	Ice Hockey	International Hockey League	Rosemont Horizon

The appreciation of European football (soccer) is in its infancy in Chicago but was helped considerably in 1998 when the home team, the **Chicago Fire**, won an important national championship game. Enthusiasm for this game, which is probably enjoyed by more spectators than any other in the world, can only be expected to increase in Chicago. The Chicago Fire plays its games at Soldier Field at present.

Amateur Sports and Fitness
Participation in sports and fitness programs provides enjoyment and social activities for many Chicagoans. Jogging, cycling, and in-line skating are all popular pursuits, as any trip to the lakefront will show you. Many professional people belong to a gym or health club where they "work out" regularly as part of a daily or weekly routine. The YMCA has several facilities in Chicagoland offering a variety of sports and fitness activities.

In-line skaters and bicyclists share a pathway along the lakefront.

Gambling

Recent laws have considerably liberalized gambling in Illinois, enabling the activity (and its promoters) to flourish. It was decided that gambling shouldn't be done on land, and so it happens on river boats. You have to leave Chicago to find most of these, but you won't have to go very far, and you won't be in Chicago for very long before you see the advertisements calling you to these places. Proposals are currently being proposed (and opposed) to allow floating casinos to ply the waters of Lake Michigan.

On a more mundane level, Illinois operates a state lottery like most states. There are daily and weekly games on which you can bid as little as a dollar and as much as your paycheck, in the hope of winning big. Details are available at the many places that sell tickets; there is one on nearly every busy corner. Finally there is horseracing in Chicagoland at five tracks. Hawthorne Race Course and Sportsman's Park, both on the southwest side, and Arlington Park Racetrack in Arlington Heights offer thoroughbred racing. They divide up the year by each taking a season, so one of them is open at any given time. Balmoral Park Racetrack in south suburban Crete has harness racing the year round; Maywood Park Racetrack in west suburban Maywood has harness racing in the spring.

MEETING CHICAGOANS

You will have the most luck in meeting other Chicagoans and developing social relationships with them if you use the same methods for meeting people that they use. The usual time-honored methods of exploiting contacts that come about naturally are the best and easiest place to start: through your work colleagues, family members, and existing friends, other parents at your children's schools, as well as people in organizations to which you belong.

Single people with more time on their hands may want to join the great number of Chicagoans who obviously find these traditional means inadequate, because a whole industry exists to put people in touch with each other who share common interests but whose paths for whatever reason have not crossed yet. The main marketplace for this industry is personal ads. It should be pointed out that at any given time only a tiny minority of people use these ads. Many more people read them than actually place them, but many adults at one time or another have either placed or responded to an ad. The *Chicago Reader* has the largest number of personal ads; other more specialized publications have ads appealing to particular tastes, and the daily newspapers run some form of personal ad service as well.

Some of these services have recordings of the person placing the ad that you can listen to; you can usually also leave your recorded message for the advertiser. A charge will appear on your telephone bill when you use the telephone numbers associated with these services. Do not be surprised at the specificity and explicitness of some personal ads; remember, America is the land of choice. You should use the same common sense and precautions when meeting someone through an ad that you would practice with a total stranger.

A common experience of foreigners among Americans is that they make friends very fast, but the friendships aren't very deep. There is probably a lot of truth to this observation. Deep friendships usually require long periods of time to cultivate and a lot of common experience between the people involved. Americans, being very mobile and very busy, are perhaps not as likely as people from many countries to have stayed in one place long enough to develop really binding friendships. It has already been pointed out that a lot of the time that Americans could in principle spend pursuing and cultivating friendships is in fact spent in pursuing and cultivating individuality and self-fulfillment. So you may find your best friends among your compatriots or among other members of the foreign community in Chicago, whose experiences will in many respects be more like yours. On the other hand, if you can learn to enjoy the sort of casual friendships with many different people that a lot of Americans enjoy, you may find the experience enriching and rewarding. We will spend a little time then looking at some of the social habits of the natives to acquaint you with their turf, starting with an easy lesson about names.

A Word About Names

The American system of using and passing on names is similar to what you find in many European countries and in most English-speaking countries, with a few variations. At birth a child is given a name chosen by the parents, called a **first name**. The child also uses the family name of his or her father, called the **last name**. Most people also have a middle name that is not typically used and is often reduced to an initial; this is what "initial" or "middle initial" means on forms that you fill out. (You should leave it blank if you don't have a middle name.)

When a woman marries she traditionally drops her family name and starts using her husband's family name, but increasingly many women retain their own family names after marriage or use it as a middle name before their husband's family name, as in Hilary Rodham Clinton. A few married couples may start to use a hyphenated name or have their children use a hyphenated name that is a combination of their two family names: thus Randy Shoals and Jennifer Courtney may have a child that goes by Heather Courtney-Shoals.

Many of the most common given names have "nicknames" associated with them that are widely used; these will be known to you already if you have a long acquaintance with English. Some people's real first name is actually the nickname form. Here is a table of common men's and women's names that have nicknames associated with them:

Man's name	Nickname	Woman's name	Nickname
Anthony	Tony	Angela	Angie
Charles	Charlie, Chuck	Barbara	Barb
Christopher	Chris	Christine	Chris
Daniel	Dan, Danny	Cynthia	Cindy
Douglas	Doug	Deborah	Debbie
Edward	Ed, Eddy	Eleanor	Elly
Edmund	Ed, Eddy	Elizabeth	Betty
Francis	Frank	Jacqueline	Jackie
Gregory	Greg	Jennifer	Jenny
Henry	Hank	Katherine	Kathy
James	Jim	Kathleen	Kathy
Kenneth	Kenny, Ken	Kimberley	Kim
Lawrence	Larry	Margaret	Peg, Peggy
Matthew	Matt	Pamela	Pam
Michael	Mike	Sandra	Sandy
Richard	Dick, Rick	Susan	Sue
Robert	Bob, Rob	Victoria	Vicki

In any social context people introduce themselves by their first names only, or by their first and last names. Initially you need remember only the first name, because this is what people expect to be called. If your name doesn't easily conform to the first-name/last-name system, you should introduce yourself by the name you want to be called. If your name is unusual or difficult to pronounce, find an English word that it sounds like or rhymes with in order to give people a handle on it; this will be appreciated. Don't be surprised if Americans very quickly reduce your name to something shorter or more familiar!

Home Life

The rich variety of ethnic heritage in Chicago, combined with the evolution that the nuclear family is currently undergoing, make it impossible to generalize about how people behave in their homes and what combinations of people you might find there. It can't quite be said that anything goes, but it may seem that Chicagoans have arrived at the step just before anything goes. For example, one household may contain children with two different fathers being raised by a third who has his own children by a former marriage, while another household may have two female parents who are raising an adopted Chinese girl in the Jewish faith. These may be unusual examples, but they are not so uncommon that you are unlikely to come across them. The transience that characterizes much of American life is now taking its turn in the family, and the term *family* has come to mean a group of people who share a household and dependent relationships. It is now quite common for men and women to set up housekeeping together without being married and to have all the trappings of a married life — sometimes including children — but no marriage license.

If circumstances such as these go strongly against the grain of your training or culture, the best advice is for you just to take it in and not react to it. Immigrants are traditionally a more conservative group than their age-peers in the native population, so Americans may in fact expect to have to explain their situations to you in greater detail than they would to another American. Remember that America is the land of choice, and that people very often choose things that aren't an option in many parts of the world. It may also be comforting to know that a great many people, especially in the suburbs, live happily within the traditional model of the nuclear family: mom, dad, and the kids.

Dining with Chicagoans

Chicagoans are as happy to eat together as people everywhere. As elsewhere in the United States, restaurant culture is endemic.

207

Friends, families, or business associates are as likely to eat out together in restaurants as they are in somebody's home. You shouldn't take it amiss if a new friend or associate asks you to dine in a restaurant rather than in their home; this is normal. General rules of etiquette are much the same in both places, but eating in someone's home is usually more intimate and relaxed than eating in a restaurant.

When you are invited to someone's home there are a few rituals (or lack thereof) that may seem unusual to you, but you can rest assured that they are simply a part of American hospitality and are not being conducted to send you some kind of subliminal message. If you are visiting someone's house for the first time, it is customary to be invited, if not strong-armed, to "take a tour," that is, see all the parts of the house. This will sometimes be done in tortured detail that includes lavatories, closets, and unfinished rooms. It is suitable for you to murmur appreciation from time to time, and if your host calls attention to some piece of decorating ingenuity or a challenging do-it-yourself project recently completed, you can marvel at it.

Most Americans do not take their shoes off in the house; they wear them everywhere. People sit in whatever way is comfortable for them, without regard to postures that may be considered offensive in some parts of the world. If someone sits with their feet pointing toward you, or exposing the bottom of their shoes, you should think nothing of it; they are not aware that it can cause offense. There is also no real protocol about where people sit in relation to each other. You should not infer anything about anyone's relative rank or status within the household according to where or how they sit.

Mind Your Manners
The general informality of American culture means that you need not be on pins and needles at the dinner table, wondering whether your way of eating is going to cause deep offense. There are,

however, a few general rules to keep in mind, as well as a few pointers applying specifically to home or restaurant dining.

Most meals are accompanied by a fork, knife, and spoon beside the plate, but the fork does most of the work. There is a slight awkwardness in American table manners in that both the knife and fork are used in the same hand (right for a right-handed person, left for a left-handed person), so that after you've cut something with your knife you have to put it down and then take the fork into the preferred hand to bring it to your mouth. There will be no offense if you eat in the European way, keeping the fork always in one hand and the knife in the other, but it may mean that you will be constantly rubbing elbows with somebody sitting at your knife-wielding side.

Many foods can be eaten with the fingers, especially in people's homes and fast-food restaurants; these include hot and cold sandwiches, fried chicken, ribs, and pizza.

Butter in the United States is sold in long, rectangular shapes called sticks. In people's homes one of these is likely to be present at the dinner table in a butter dish. The correct way to serve yourself is to slice vertically from one end of the stick, using your clean table knife or a butter knife provided. Do not scrape your knife across the top of the stick; this will be regarded as quite barbaric.

It is better not to even ask if you can smoke in somebody's home if you have already observed that no one else is smoking. Many people today simply do not permit smoking indoors, and it may be awkward for them to refuse you. If, on the other hand, you have spotted ashtrays about, you should ask if you can smoke before you light up.

Talking the Talk

The United States has what specialists in the field like to call a "low-context" culture. A high proportion of what is communicated is made explicit in language and does not depend on the listener making arcane inferences or having to be well-versed in significant

209

but ambiguous looks, gestures, or other clues. Urban culture is probably even lower in context than the general culture, since it so often draws together people of varying backgrounds who cannot be expected to be conversant in the secret ways of other speakers and listeners. All this is very much to the advantage of the foreigner in Chicago. It means that you don't run the risk of making a fool of yourself or of saying or doing something deeply embarrassing because nobody bothered to tell you that such things just aren't said or done.

Long before you set foot in somebody's house you will have probably already noticed the tendency of Americans to "get personal" very early on, sharing bits of themselves with you in conversation that you do not have any real need to know, and asking you personal questions about things you may well feel are none of their business. Your presence in somebody's home is a green light for your host to proceed farther down this road. If you have not met other members of your host's family (spouse, children, and the like), they may have questions for you too. Asking questions and sharing personal information is the fast-track American way of "getting to know" somebody. You are not obliged to reciprocate by asking a lot of questions yourself—indeed, you may not have to because volumes of information may be volunteered—but to the extent that you are comfortable with providing personal information about yourself, you will be regarded as likable and friendly.

A popular perception of Americans among foreigners is their insularity, manifested not so much in a lack of openness as in a studied disinterest in what goes on in the rest of the world beyond their borders. The reasons for this phenomenon are the business of the sociologist, but the effects of it will be very much of concern to you and probably obvious to you from the outset if you have not lived in the United States before. You should not be surprised to find Chicagoans quite ignorant about where you come from; even if they know where it is, they may be unfamiliar with the social, political, and economic issues that are paramount in your country. They may ask you questions about your country but then stop you short if you start to give a complicated answer!

While Americans are very expressive verbally and are responsible for coining many of the liveliest words and phrases in English, they are not necessarily as articulate in English as people with equal education from other English-speaking countries. There is an underemphasis on developing speaking and debating skills in American schools, and the approach to proper grammar and usage is much less rigorous than in many countries. The result is that you may find American speech not only difficult to understand but also fraught with small errors and not very carefully considered. You should not assume from this that Americans are any less intelligent than other native speakers of English. Americans place greater emphasis on informality than they do on correct speech; it is a way of crossing barriers and reaching out to others. Politicians, especially, often practice "dumbing-down" or colloquializing their speech. A case in point was a dedication ceremony of a statue in one of Chicago's parks many years ago, attended by Mayor Richard J. Daley, the commissioner of the Park District, and the King of Sweden. All three addressed the audience, but only the King of Sweden spoke in complete sentences and without grammatical errors!

There are no real conversational taboos in American culture other than the ones that prevail universally. Talk about sex, religion, and politics generally carries the same warning labels that it bears everywhere, but all three are discussed with enthusiasm by people well known to one another. Because of the very strong feelings that exist on both sides of the issue, it is inadvisable to enter into a discussion about abortion, unless it is in a private setting with one person whom you know very well. You can ask the price or cost of anything without fear of being thought too

211

forward or prying, unless there is a great disparity of incomes or means between speaker and listener.

Forty percent of the world's Jewish population lives in the United States. By contrast, the proportion of Americans with ties to Middle Eastern countries other than Israel is quite small. As a result, you may find American media coverage and political policies in the Middle East quite biased. If you have strong feelings on this subject, it is a good one to avoid in group conversations.

It may be helpful to have a brief lesson in the prevailing mood of "political correctness" that grips America, so that you don't unwittingly make mistakes in referring to people. The greatest sensitivity in this regard centers around terms for people who are perceived as constituting a minority of some kind: people of various nationalities and ethnic groups, people with handicaps, gay people. In general it is acceptable to refer to people's nationality by the standard adjective derived from the associated noun of the country; thus you may say Polish for someone from Poland, Vietnamese for someone from Vietnam, Argentinean for someone from Argentina. There are a few terms in currency from other parts of the English-speaking world that no longer pass in America. Here is a list of terms to avoid if possible with their acceptable equivalents:

- Jew (not generally offensive, but the adjective "Jewish" is preferred)
- Negro (use "black" or "African-American," according to context)
- Red Indian (use "Native American" or "American Indian")

Your experience would be very unusual indeed if you did not hear various other terms that refer to people of different nationalities. All-male conversations are particularly rich in the use of terms that characterize ethnic and minority groups either humorously or disparagingly. It may be tempting to fall into the use of such terms as a way of belonging to a group, since such stereotyping of others is often a way that groups define themselves.

A few other points may help you to say the right thing at the right time when talking with Chicagoans, especially those whom you don't know well.

- When looking for a toilet in someone's home you can ask for the *restroom* or *bathroom*. These terms can also be used in public places, along with *men's room* or *ladies' room*.
- People with disabilities of various kinds may be called just that: *people with disabilities*. The specific terminology for different afflictions is in flux now with a number of terms contending for domination. It is probably not worth cataloguing them, but do avoid some of the terms that are now regarded as old-fashioned and disparaging: *retarded, mentally retarded, crippled, lame*.
- *Gay* is an acceptable term for homosexual people of either sex, and *lesbian* is acceptable for homosexual women. Just about all the other terms you know are probably considered offensive.

Fatal Gestures

Americans are not as likely to communicate unambiguously by gesture as people in many other cultures, but there are a small number of gestures whose meaning is always clear and these you might find useful to know. A loose fist with the thumb pointing upward, as well as the expression "thumbs up," is a sign of approval; a loose fist with the thumb pointing downward is a sign of rejection or disapproval, as is the expression "thumbs down." These phrases are the stock-in-trade of the two well-known Chicago movie critics, Roger Ebert and Gene Siskell, whose dual approval is often critical to the success of commercially released films. Forming a circle with the thumb and forefinger is also a sign of approval, or an indication to somebody that they have done a good job. A raised middle finger with the palm toward the gesturer is a rude and aggressive insult that you should never use. Drivers may flash this gesture if you do something to anger them. It is best to ignore it.

The Life of the Party

Fairly early on in your Chicago life you will probably be invited to a party of some kind, through connections with your work, neighbors, or friends. Urban Americans, especially single people, have fairly frequent gatherings that fall under the heading of "party," and there doesn't really have to be a significant occasion to hold one, although an occasion of some kind, even if contrived, is normally given. When weather permits people have outdoor parties, usually called barbecues, whether or not food is actually cooked in this fashion. Other occasions for parties include weddings, birthdays, promotions, moving into a new house (a "housewarming" party), or any number of other less important events. A number of American holidays, both major and minor, are often occasions for parties, such as the Fourth of July or Labor Day. Among some of Chicago's ethnic communities unofficial holidays are occasions for parties: St. Patrick's Day for the Irish, Columbus Day for the Italians, and so forth.

The etiquette connected with various kinds of parties varies considerably. For specific details it is probably a good idea for you to consult another person who is going to the same party or the host for specifics about what sort of clothes to wear, whether you should bring anything to eat or drink, whether you can or should bring a guest, and the like. Chances are that your host will volunteer some of this information, but if it is not forthcoming, don't hesitate to ask. Except for weddings, Americans tend to dress casually and comfortably for any sort of party. At informal parties where food is served, it is usually suitable for you to bring something to the party that can be consumed, either food or drink. A party advertised as "BYOB" means bring your own booze; it doesn't mean you have to bring an alcoholic beverage, just bring something that you like to drink. Suburbanites may sometimes participate in a "potluck" dinner, where everyone brings a dish and all share the food communally. This is often associated with church social groups. Proper Chicagoans, however, would probably find this idea a bit rustic.

It is a rare party that *doesn't* include alcoholic drinks among urban Americans, but there are a significant number of people today who don't drink. You will not be out of place if you choose not to drink. Although drinks flow freely, many people object to cigarette smoke, so you should not assume that you can light up indoors unless you see others doing so. Typically smokers at a private party gather from time to time in cliques outside where they can have a cigarette, or in some designated area away from others where their smoke will not be disturbing.

Parties are one area of American life where it is OK to be "fashionably late." You can show up at a party any time from the advertised starting time onward, but most people come about half an hour late. If the party is advertised as having definite starting and stopping times — 3 p.m. to 7 p.m., for example — it means that the host really does want everyone out by the "closing" time. It is even acceptable for a host to "chase everybody out" (ask politely that they leave) if the party has a definite ending time. Remember, for Americans the clock is always ticking.

The American attributes of individualism and initiative are very much in evidence at parties and you shouldn't expect anybody to "lead you by the hand," even if you are new to Chicago or to the particular group of people at the party. Your host or someone who knows you may introduce you to one or two people, but for most of the time you are likely to be on your own, like everyone else. The expected thing to do is to "mingle," introducing yourself to people that you think look interesting. People at parties normally engage in what Americans call "small talk," which is conversation about topics that are not likely to arouse great emotions and can be talked about in a friendly and humorous way. It is also perfectly acceptable at most parties to "network," that is, to find and talk to people who may be useful to you in your work or professional life. Even if you meet somebody at a party in whom you are very interested, it is probably better not to try to monopolize the person and give them no opportunity to socialize with others. Arrange another meeting with them at a later time if you feel you have a lot more to talk about.

Food and drink service at parties is also informal. You may be given your first drink, but thereafter you'll probably be told where the makings are and you can serve yourself. Food is typically served buffet style, from a large table, where everyone fills his own plate and munches on food while chatting with others.

Short Social Occasions and Rituals

Many foreigners are amazed—and sometimes hurt—by the small amount of time that Americans can devote to a single social occasion and still think of it as such. In many parts of the world it would be unthinkable to be a guest in a person's home and stay less than a few hours. Both the guest and the host could take offense or could be considered rude if such a thing were to happen. Not so in American cities where everything happens on the fast track. If someone says they are coming over, or if they invite you over, to "drop something off," it means just that; it is not a pretext for a longer social call. Remember that Americans plan and budget time as a commodity: a thing that exists in limited quantity and therefore is to be parceled out as efficiently as possible.

The principle of "fast is best" applies equally to various ritual forms of communication. Though it may take some getting used to, you will eventually view this American trait as a blessing in disguise. You are not required to learn any lengthy greeting or parting rituals, nor to suffer through any. Americans are ready to "get down to business" after the briefest exchange of greetings. The questions "How are you?" or "How's it going?" don't really want a detailed answer, unless there is or has been something wrong with you. You will be rending the social fabric if you use a friendly greeting of this kind as an opportunity to go on at length

216

about your hardships. Similarly, when it's time to say goodbye, that's what you do. There is no need to make an allusion to parting until you are actually ready to go, because once you do, everything changes. Then there is really nothing left for you to do but say goodbye, with perhaps a reference to your next meeting, if there is to be one, and an acknowledgment of the enjoyment of your time together.

YOUR MEDIA DIET

However social your leisure time, you are likely to fill some of it with "downtime," simply relaxing at home and taking advantage of the soothing regimen of television, radio, magazines, and newspapers. Here is a brief guide to what you can expect to find in Chicago.

Americans' (and Chicagoans') preoccupation with domestic matters is reflected in the news media. The national TV networks, though they may purport to report "world news," give far more air-time to domestic matters than international ones. Newspapers are even more parochial; the Chicago dailies (discussed below) devote a lot more banner headlines and column inches to local stories than to national or international ones. Radio networks are perhaps the worst offenders of all in their ignorance of international affairs. They select, from among all events unfolding on the planet, to report mostly on those involving lurid crimes, litigation, and scandals connected with private individuals throughout the United States.

This means that if you want to keep informed about life in the world and maintain a balanced perspective on international events, you will have to shop for your sources of information, rather than mindlessly consuming the ones that come at you. Fortunately there are good options available. Here is a summary of what you can find, and what is likely to find you, floating in the sea of current information around Chicago.

Television
Chicagoland has 14 television stations, representing the national networks, public television stations (described below), and various other foreign language (mostly Spanish), independent, and special purpose channels. This is only the beginning of the story. Nearly anywhere you live in Chicagoland you can easily get access to cable television, which will deliver 70–100 channels to your screen. Every area of Chicagoland is served by a cable company that has exclusive license to that area. You pay a monthly subscription fee that entitles you to all the basic, and if you pay extra, the premium channels handled by that company. You will be amazed at how much of this audiovisual torrent is sheer blather, seemingly designed to waste your time and distract you from the more important things in life! If you subscribe to cable television, you will very likely overdose on it early on and eventually settle into a pattern of using it judiciously. Be warned that it is a major distraction that ever promises satisfaction but rarely delivers it.

With the exception of some premium (i.e., extra cost) cable channels, there is in effect no commercial-free television in the United States. Public television stations—of which there are two in Chicagoland (nominally channels 11 and 20, though they may be received on other channels according to your cable company's configuration)—carry sponsorship messages rather than commercials. These are supposed to be shorter and less offensive than commercials, but it's getting hard to tell the difference. Public TV is partly supported by subscriptions from the public. If you enjoy their programming it is a good idea to support them by becoming a member. They have the best quality programming available.

Other television stations, including the national networks, syndicated cable stations, and special purpose cable stations (such as news channels, the Weather Channel, sports channels, Court TV, music channels, and the like) all carry a heavy dose of advertising. Some channels, such as shopping channels, consist of nothing but advertising. Most people find it useful to own a VCR to tape programs and thus have the option to fast-forward through the commercials when viewing the programs. It is worth noting that TVs and VCRs manufactured in other parts of the world will probably not work in the United States. VCRs use a format called VHS that is not compatible with the PAL system used in Europe and Asia.

Radio

More than 100 radio stations can be received in Chicago, divided more or less equally between the FM and AM bands. AM, for amplitude modulation, is often called MW, or medium wave, elsewhere in the English-speaking world. Only stations on FM can broadcast in stereo, so the stations that are more serious about music, whether it be classical, country-western, or rock and roll, are on the FM band.

Also on the FM band is NPR, or National Public Radio. The Chicago station is WBEZ at 91.5. If you live in the western suburbs you may be able to pick up WNIV on 89.5, another Chicagoland NPR station. This is the closest thing you'll get to BBC-type news and public affairs broadcasting, with little commercial interruption, though it does carry the same sort of sponsorship messages that air on public television. NPR stations are supported not only by corporate sponsors but by listeners. Most of them hold twice-yearly fund-raising weeks, during which listeners are asked to pay a subscription. If you listen to these stations, it is a good idea to support them; they provide the best, least biased, and most intelligently presented news coverage. They are far superior in international coverage to network radio. Many of them use correspondents and reports from Britain-based news organizations in their coverage.

The AM radio band is a hodgepodge of talk radio, popular music, sports, news, and special interest broadcasts, including broadcasts in many foreign languages at different times of day.

219

The national television networks own counterpart radio stations whose news coverage is probably the worst and most parochial available with frequent, loud, and offensive commercial interruptions.

As for the rest of the radio band, longwave and shortwave broadcast is not as highly developed in the United States as abroad. Nevertheless, many foreign and international stations can be picked up if you have a good receiver and live on the outskirts of the metropolitan area, away from the built-up center of town. Shortwave and longwave reception is quite poor in the city unless you invest in expensive receiving and aerial equipment. The BBC World Service broadcasts in English to the United States on shortwave frequencies in the 16, 31, and 49 meter bands. Look for updates to frequency and schedule details on the BBC's World Service website, **www.bbc.co.uk/worldservice**.

Print Media

Chicago has two main daily newspapers, the *Chicago Tribune* (**www.chicagotribune.com**) and the *Chicago Sun-Times* (**www. suntimes.com**). Their daily circulation combined is just over a million, with the *Tribune* currently and historically keeping a significant lead. Both also publish Sunday editions (for sale from Saturday morning onward) that are bloated with supplemental advertising. On Sunday the *Tribune's* circulation is more than double that of the *Sun-Times*. Neither Chicago daily is as good as some of the country's east coast dailies, for example the *New York Times* (**www.nytimes.com**) or *Washington Post* (**www.washingtonpost. com**). The Chicago papers' focus is unabashedly parochial and sensational by comparison to these two newspapers. For this reason many educated Chicagoans prefer to take the *New York Times* as their daily paper. It is widely available from newsstands, street vending boxes, and by subscription.

The United States' only official national daily, *USA Today* (**www.usatoday.com**), is also widely available from all these locations. It is aimed at the middle-brow reader who likes lots of color pictures and not too much in-depth analysis.

Readers who take a special interest in business affairs and economic issues will want to read the *Wall Street Journal* (**www. wsj.com**), a New York-based daily that is published nationally and covers all the most important news with a strong emphasis on its economic impact. It has the most complete securities and commodities market reports and analysis. It is available by sub-scription, from newsstands, and from street vending boxes.

In addition, there are more than 50 neighborhood and spe-cial interest newspapers published on a daily, weekly, or monthly basis for nearly every segment of Chicago's community. Some notable titles are listed below.

Chicago Magazine (**www.chicagomag.com**) is a monthly "good living" magazine of the sort that every major city has. It includes arts listings, feature articles, glossy advertising, and restaurant reviews.

The *Chicago Reader* (**www.chicagoreader.com**) is distributed free throughout Chicagoland every Friday (you can get it Thursday afternoon if you want to beat the rush). The *Reader* is a four-section tabloid that has the most complete arts and entertainment listings in the city, as well as free and paid want ads covering every possible need and desire. The bulk of the paper is advertis-ing, but there are a few interesting columns and cartoons that have avid followers, as well as a lengthy, in-depth cover article every week.

Crain's Chicago Business (**www.crainschicagobusiness.com**) is a weekly indispensable tool for the successful capitalist, whether established or aspiring.

New City (**www.newcitychicago.com**) is another widely distrib-uted free weekly with significant arts coverage, advertising, and feature articles. It is more selective and much easier to get through than the *Reader.*

Streetwise (**www.streetwise.org**) is a weekly tabloid sold by and for the benefit of homeless people. It takes a more left-wing view of social issues than the mainstream media would ever dare and generally favors the underdog. Standing features include a very complete listing of helplines and crisis intervention lines in Chicago, as well as a listing of charities that accept donated goods and organizations that need volunteer help.

The ***Windy City Times***, another free weekly, is aimed at Chicago's gay and lesbian community. It is distributed in gay venues, bookstores, college campuses, and many other retail establishments in gay neighborhoods such as Lake View.

A national magazine that may be of particular interest to the foreigner or newcomer in Chicago is ***Consumer Reports***. It is a monthly publication available by subscription, at news dealers, and also in most public libraries. *Consumer Reports* impartially rates all kinds of consumer products, from irons and toasters to cars and life insurance. It issues an annual buying guide, sent free to subscribers, that summarizes its findings on the major categories of products. Both the magazine and the annual buying guide are very useful to anyone who will be making numerous purchases for a household.

If you're looking for newspapers from other parts of the world, especially those in other languages, first try the ethnic and specialty food stores listed in chapter 6; they often carry a selection of newspapers and magazines from the part of the world that their food is from. A few of the larger newsagents downtown and on the Near North Side have a selection of foreign dailies, mostly European ones.

THE HOLIDAYS

We conclude this chapter with an overview of the customs surrounding various holidays and the ways in which you may have an opportunity to participate in them with Chicagoans. Holidays in general are occasions that people like to spend with their families, since most people aren't working and it is a chronic complaint of Americans that they don't have enough time with their families. Since people often live quite far from close members of their family, holidays frequently involve travel, and airports are busier in the holiday season than at any other time of year.

When Americans talk about **the holidays** without any further qualification, they mean the two big ones that fall close together—Christmas and New Year—or they may include in this Thanksgiving as well, which comes at the end of November. This entire period, from Thanksgiving until the new year, is sometimes loosely called the **holiday season**, although this term can also refer more narrowly to the time around Christmas. It is a good place to begin our discussion since these are the holidays most cherished by nearly all Americans.

Thanksgiving is the most family-centered of all U.S. holidays, when everyone traditionally goes home or to the home of relatives to give thanks for their good fortune, however great or small. It is not a religious holiday per se and for that reason it draws together Americans of all religions. This American holiday was first celebrated by early European settlers who had survived their first year of trying conditions in the New World and wanted to offer thanks. The centerpiece of the holiday is the Thanksgiving Day meal, traditionally of stuffed, roast turkey accompanied by a glut of side dishes and finished off with pumpkin pie.

A stereotype of the holiday is for men to spend the afternoon watching football on television, although there are many who don't. Everyone is more or less expected to spend Thanksgiving Day with someone in their family; it is one of the few times

223

when it is not considered suitable, or at the very least is considered quite pitiable, to be alone. If you don't have the opportunity to spend the holiday with your family, you may well be invited to dine with Americans, to spare you the plight of being on your own.

Christmas has come quite a long way from being the festival set aside to celebrate Christ's birth. Its main manifestation now is a consumerist orgy of gift-giving and overeating. At the same time there is a strong emphasis from some quarters to restore the religious aspects of the holiday, so in fact it is a kind of omnibus holiday that carries baggage of all kinds. The Jewish holiday of **Hanukkah** falls around the same time as Christmas and is given a seat in the holiday vehicle that roars through December. Likewise for **Kwanza**, a recently invented holiday to celebrate the country's African-American heritage.

Regardless of their religious or ethnic affiliation, nearly all Americans celebrate Christmas or at least make some gesture toward it. Gift-giving is standard among family and friends, and sometimes in work environments as well. Colleagues may exchange gifts, and any bonuses in pay or salary that a company gives its workers is usually given at this time of year. The focus of Christmas for many people is children, and the focus of the children is the ecumenical figure of **Santa Claus,** who is on hand in multiple incarnations to learn what gifts they would like to receive and to distribute them. Gifts are opened on Christmas Eve (evening of December 24) or on Christmas Day. A big festive meal is also a traditional feature of Christmas Day.

New Year's Eve is a holiday to be cherished or avoided like the plague, depending on what your idea of fun is. Loud noisy parties are the rule, and it is mandatory to stay up until midnight in order to "ring in" the New Year and, if you're at the right kind of party, kiss everyone in sight. Those who wish to avoid all this simply lock their doors and stay home. Chicago doesn't have a fixed out-door celebration of the arrival of the New Year since it is very likely to be numbingly cold at this time of year.

The next cluster of holidays that you may want to be aware of are those connected with **Easter,** the Christian holiday that marks Christ's death and resurrection. Only religious Christians empha-size this aspect of the holiday, and for many Americans it passes without observation at all since there are no official days off from work associated with it. Children dye and decorate hard-cooked eggs, and some adults hide colored eggs so that the children may engage in an Easter Egg Hunt. Sweets of all kinds are a feature of the holiday as well, in the form of chocolate bunnies and candy eggs. Unless you have children or wish to participate in the reli-gious aspects of the holiday, this is probably one that you can give a miss. The Wednesday before Easter is **Ash Wednesday**, when some Catholics mark their foreheads with a cross of ashes; it is the only day in the year when you should not think it remarkable to see people on the street with black smudges on their foreheads. The Jewish holiday season of **Passover** traditionally falls around the same time as Easter.

The only remaining holiday that deserves special mention because of its pure American origins is the **Fourth of July**, also called **Independence Day**. It celebrates the day in 1776 when American colonialists, then ruled by Britain, ratified the Declara-tion of Independence and thus began the revolution that led to the emergence of the United States as a sovereign country. Most Americans, however much complaining they may do, are indel-ibly patriotic and love their country. The Fourth of July is the day for them to wear their patriotism proudly, so it is a loud and happy affair. Outdoor barbecues are traditional, as well as evening parties in places that afford views of one of the many fireworks displays around.

225

CHAPTER ELEVEN

APPENDICES

There are some cities that are resolutely turned toward the future. Chicago is one of them. Its very size, the beauty of its bold modern architecture —these are the signs of a powerful dynamic metropolis full of life and activity.

— Jacques Chirac

A. THE CHICAGO CALENDAR

The list here is of U.S. national holidays, holidays with special meaning in Chicagoland, and religious holidays that affect a majority of Chicagoans in one way or another. Most of the lesser official holidays are marked by the retail trade as opportunities for sales of various kinds, thus turning them into celebrations of materialism, which is perhaps one of the most enduring American traditions!

You will also find noted many special events that occur at predictable times throughout the year, and events fixed by various seasons that have a bearing on Chicagoans' lives. This does *not* attempt to be a comprehensive guide to what's going on in Chicago at any particular time, because there is always more going on than any one person can possibly be aware of. To get some feel for current events, there are a couple of good websites: the Chicago calendar of events operated by the *Chicago Sun-Times* on their website, **www.suntimes.com/calendar,** and the calendar on the City of Chicago's official website, **www.ci.chi.il.us/tourism/ calendar.** A visit to this website is strongly recommended as the best place to get an overall view of every conceivable thing about Chicago; it is a virtual electronic encyclopedia devoted to the city. You can also call the Mayor's Office of Special Events [(312) 744-3315] to find out what's current at any time of year.

January

The year begins with an official holiday, **New Year's Day.** Most businesses are closed. January 15 is the birthday of **Dr. Martin Luther King**, the slain civil rights leader. It is officially celebrated on the third Monday in the month, thus making for a three-day weekend, but it is the least observed of all official holidays and is not a day off for many workers, unless employed at some level of government or by the U.S. Postal Service. Toward the end of the month, with unavoidable media fanfare, comes **Superbowl Sunday**, the Sunday on which the championship game in American football is played. Fans of the game typically have parties to watch the game on television, accompanied by much shouting, drink, and emotion.

February

February 2 is **Groundhog Day**, an unofficial and frivolous American holiday on which it is said that the groundhog, a large

227

burrowing rodent native to eastern North America, predicts the course of the remainder of the winter. If it emerges from hibernation and sees its shadow, winter will continue for another six weeks; if it sees no shadow, spring will arrive early. Of course it is all nonsense, but the media and schoolchildren have fun with the holiday. February 14 is **Valentine's Day,** a day when people show appreciation for their loved ones with cards or gifts, traditionally flowers or chocolate. Two of America's most famous presidents were born in February: Illinois' own Abraham Lincoln on February 12, and George Washington on February 22. These are combined into **President's Day** on the third Monday of the month, making another three-day weekend. Aside from government workers and schoolchildren, the holiday is not widely observed. The **Chinese New Year** is usually celebrated in February with lavish parades and festivities in Chinatown.

The whole month of February is **African-American History Month.** Look for special events at the Cultural Center and at the DuSable Museum on E. 56th Street.

March
Though not an official holiday, **St. Patrick's Day** on March 17 is one of the most festive days on Chicago's calendar, owing to the many people of Irish descent in Chicagoland, and partly to the domination of city government by Irish politicians for most of this century. There is a major parade down Dearborn Street, the Chicago River is dyed green for the day, and beer is tinted green in many bars. It is also tradition to wear something green; if you don't, it is license for others to pinch you!

April
April Fool's Day is the first day of the month; as elsewhere in the English-speaking world, Chicago celebrates the day with pranks and practical jokes, though these are usually not carried to the extremes seen in the United Kingdom or Australia. If they did not

occur in March, the movable Christian holidays of **Good Friday** and **Easter Sunday** occur sometime in April. Neither of these is a holiday in the United States, nor is the Monday following, as it is in many Christian countries. The Jewish holiday of **Passover** also occurs near the time of Easter.

The baseball season officially begins, but unless you're comfortable with the possibility of developing blue lips, wait until the weather warms up a little before going to watch any games at Wrigley Field or Comiskey Park.

May

The second Sunday of the month is **Mother's Day,** not an official holiday but a day when people show appreciation for their mothers (also wives and grandmothers) with gifts, cards, and family celebrations. May 30 is **Memorial Day**; it is officially celebrated on the final Monday of the month, making for another three-day weekend. The day was set aside originally to honor Civil War dead, later extended to honor all war dead; lately, it is mainly an occasion for blowout sales at major department stores. Not to be excluded from Chicago's parade-mania, the Poles have their day on or around May 3, with a Dearborn Street parade that celebrates **Polish Constitution Day.** Later in the month, around the 25th, the Greeks get their turn with the **Greek-American parade** down Michigan Avenue. **Cinco de Mayo**, Spanish for 5th of May, commemorates a 19th century Mexican military victory and is celebrated in a big way in Latino neighborhoods starting at the end of April.

The **Stanley Cup playoffs**, hockey's championship series, usually takes place in early May. By the end of May, the city is cranking up for the various **neighborhood festivals** and **music festivals** (jazz, blues, gospel, country, Latino) that happen in succession the whole summer long. School is out for most schoolchildren by the end of the month.

Volunteers hand refreshments to runners in the Chicago marathon as they pass the Elks Memorial.

June

The third Sunday of the month is **Father's Day,** not an official holiday but a day when people show appreciation for their fathers (also husbands and grandfathers) with gifts, cards, and family celebrations. Around the middle of the month the **Ravinia Festival** starts with popular and high-culture music, and dance and theater events throughout the summer in the Northwest suburb of Highland Park. **Taste of Chicago** is an annual food festival along Columbus Drive in Grant Park. Restaurateurs and others offer (relatively) small quantities of food for considerably less than you would pay for a restaurant meal, thus allowing you to "eat your way" through. You will probably still end up eating twice as much as you would have otherwise, because so many things look and smell irresistible. It is one of the largest attractions in Chicago, with more than 3 million visitors. Musical acts and other attractions accompany it.

The **NBA playoffs** (that's basketball) take place in June, and it's a rare year that the Chicago Bulls are not playing for the championship.

July

American patriotism culminates in the **Fourth of July,** also known as **Independence Day.** Toward the end of the month, **Venetian Night,** a peculiarly Chicago festival, is celebrated on the lake with a fantastic, all-out fireworks display over Lake Michigan, which caps off a boat parade modeled on those imagined to take place in Venice. About half a million people attend, making the lakefront a bit jammed; a more fashionable view is afforded from a boat or a lakefront high-rise apartment.

August

Those who have not taken their summer vacation yet have to hurry to do so now, because by the end of the month the new **school year** has begun for children in public schools. Some colleges and universities don't start until September. This is the most expensive time of year for air travel and there are few bargains to be had. Holiday resorts are likewise packed. Chicago, being a holiday destination for millions, is also chock-a-block with tourists.

September

The first Monday of the month is **Labor Day,** the traditional end of the summer season and the last three-day weekend until November for most workers. A picnic or barbecue is the preferred activity if weather permits, and it usually does. The usual over-hyped sales in the major stores are a regular feature of the weekend as well.

Those who feel Chicago's German heritage is not adequately celebrated may want to take in the **Von Steuben Day Parade** on Dearborn Street, on the Saturday nearest September 17.

The regular football season begins and runs until December. An outing to Soldier Field to see the **Chicago Bears** in action can be a perfect all-American autumn afternoon.

October

Italian-American Chicagoans in particular mark **Columbus Day,** officially October 12 but celebrated on the Monday closest to it by those who recognize it as official and give a day off work. It is thus a three-day weekend for the select few, namely government and Postal Service workers. There is an important parade on Dearborn Street that celebrates the Italian heritage of Chicago. The last day of the month, October 31, is **Halloween**, mainly a children's holiday but one not to be ignored, in light of the fact that Americans spend more money observing it than any holiday other than Christmas. Children circulate in their neighborhood or building in costume, ringing doorbells and crying "trick or treat," to elicit a gift of candy. If you have children you will learn all you need to know and more about this holiday from them. If you don't

Pompom girls march down Dearborn Street in the Columbus Day parade.

have children but live in an area where they are likely to call, have some Halloween candy on hand to dispense. At different times during the month **Oktoberfest** is very much in the air among Chicagoans of German extraction.

The regular baseball season ends and the "**World Series**," really the national baseball championship, is played, in the home cities of the two finalist teams. Chicagoans dream of a "subway series" that would pit the Chicago White Sox against the Chicago Cubs. This hasn't happened since 1906. The White Sox last played in a World Series in 1959, and the Cubs' last World Series appearance was in 1989. Just as the baseball season ends, the basketball and hockey seasons begin and all allegiances shift to the United Center where the Chicago Bulls and Chicago Blackhawks play. The **Chicago Marathon** is also run in October, along lines similar to the marathons in other major cities around the world.

November

In a year when there are **elections** of any kind, they are normally held on the first Tuesday in November. More important elections are in even years. Years divisible by four (2000, 2004, etc.) mark elections for the U.S. President, many U.S. Senate seats, and many state and local officials. November 11 is **Veteran's Day**, set aside to honor all veterans of the armed services but not an official holiday, except for Postal Service and government workers. **Thanksgiving** is celebrated on the fourth Thursday of the month. The Friday following Thanksgiving is a day off for most people except those in essential services and in the retail trade. It is the official beginning of the Christmas shopping season, and a good time to avoid the Loop and North Michigan Avenue, unless you like the press of flesh. On the other hand, the Christmas lights and decorations on the streets and in the windows of Loop and Near North shops are certainly worth a visit some time; the window displays of Marshall Field's are an annual achievement in decorative art.

December

All sights are set on **Christmas** on December 25. You would have to be lacking all senses to be unaware of its approach since the retail world goes mad, but amid all the noise and waste there are pleasant enjoyments like concerts of Christmas music and cheerfully decorated Christmas trees in people's homes. The last day of the year, **New Year's Eve,** is a day that typically ends early for working people so they can get ready for partying. Public transportation is free after a certain hour, to discourage people from driving under the influence of alcohol.

B. PACKING AND SHIPPING

Make sure you bring with you:

- All of your clothes for the hottest and coldest weather. Chicago's climate is one of extremes.
- Official documentation for any vital events in your life: passport or travel documents, birth certificate, marriage certificate, evidence of divorce or parenthood, medical records, U.S. visa.

The following items are not useful in Chicago or they are things that you cannot bring into the United States without undergoing lengthy formalities, owing to customs regulations:

- electrical appliances, unless they are 110 to 120 v, 50-60 Hz.
- food products that are not in sealed containers (this includes fresh fruit and vegetables)
- live or dead plants, cuttings, or seeds
- gold
- meat
- firearms and ammunition
- live animals, including pets

If you are coming to Chicago to take up an executive or other skilled position, try to get your employer to make some provision for you to ship your personal goods. If you have to pay to ship your goods yourself, it is advantageous to keep the volume to a minimum. Consumer goods of all kinds are readily available and relatively inexpensive in Chicago. It will be cheaper for you to replace many items than to ship them. For items that you must ship, find a reputable shipper in your country.

You will probably have the option of shipping goods only as far as the port of destination—you should specify Chicago for this—or you can pay to have goods delivered to your door in Chicagoland. The latter is a lot more expensive, vastly more convenient, but a little tricky if you don't have an address yet.

If you ship your goods to the port only, you will have to clear the goods through Customs yourself and pick them up from the warehouse of the receiving company. This could be anywhere in Chicagoland and is likely to be in an unfamiliar and possibly not very inviting area of the city. Both of these are quite time-consuming activities, but if you expect to have more time than money on your hands, it's the way to go.

C. PRIORITY LIST FOR SETTLING IN CHICAGO

This list sets out in a logical order the things you should think about for your move to Chicago. Don't be intimidated by it! You don't have to accomplish it in one day, and many of the items you may well be able to leave off, depending on your particular needs. The order is intended to ensure that you don't find yourself needing to do something or get something that depends entirely on something else that you haven't yet done or got.

If you have colleagues, friends, or family already in the Chicago area your affairs can be considerably facilitated by them. Short of that, there is probably no better friend than the online Chicago telephone directories (**http://yp.ameritech.net**) to help you find and contact businesses and organizations in the Chicago area.

1. Put in order the documentation that is the basis of your residency in Chicago; without this, you won't get past the Immigration officer!
2. Arrange for shipment of your personal belongings. These normally go by sea and can take one to three months in transit, depending on how far they are traveling.
3. Take steps to secure your accommodation in Chicago.
4. Buy a short health insurance policy abroad to cover the time that you will be in Chicago before you are covered by a regular policy or health plan here.
5. Apply for a Social Security number (see chapter 8).
6. Secure some U.S. currency for your journey to and arrival in Chicago. You shouldn't need more than $100 for incidental expenses. Try to have this in a variety of bills, including some $1 bills for tips and the like.
7. Open a checking account with a Chicagoland bank. If at all possible, get a credit card and an ATM card from the bank as well.
8. If you already drive and have a valid license from another country, apply for an Illinois driver's license (see chapter 3). If you don't have a valid foreign driver's license or don't intend to get a U.S. driver's license immediately, apply for an official state identification card from the Illinois Secretary of State's office.
9. Investigate health insurance coverage if it is not provided for you through your job or school.

ABOUT THE AUTHOR

Orin Hargraves is the author of *Culture Shock! Morocco* and *London At Your Door* (also entitled *Living and Working Abroad: London*). He has spent eight years of his life in Chicago, variously occupied as a toddler, university student, taxi driver, microfilm printer, hotel clerk, and technical writer. Today he lives in rural Maryland and works primarily as a lexicographer. His email address is orinkh@ccpl.carr.org

INDEX